HIGH PRAISE

THE FRESHLY .... *sing Girls in Bohemia: Meditations of an American Father,* were .... when first published individually in literary magazines. Richard Katrovas vividly conveys the complexity of the relationship between a father and his bilingual daughters who are being raised as citizens of two very different cultures. But to read these essays together adds a welcome sense of an overarching narrative, and dials the level of complexity higher still. The result is a vital, one-of-a-kind book.

    STUART DYBEK, author of *The Coast of Chicago*

A POTENT, fascinating book.

    TRACY KIDDER, author of *Strength in What Remains*

SOMETIMES A PERSON is in the right place at the right time to witness history, which is lucky. Sometimes that person is a writer of Richard Katrovas's talent, which is even luckier. These twenty-three essays reflect on a world bent on transforming itself, gazed through the transformative eye of fatherhood. From his unique position—one foot in the Bohemia of the French Quarter, one in, well, Bohemia, Katrovas speaks with humor and authority, whether describing the "Worst Restaurant in the Western World," or realizing that "My daughters are more physically free in Europe, and more rhetorically free in America." *Raising Girls in Bohemia* is a clear-eyed, sure-handed, big-hearted book.

    BETH ANN FENNELLY, author of *Great with Child*

A REMARKABLE ACHIEVEMENT, a heady ride, wise and knowing.

    PATRICIA HAMPL, author of *A Romantic Education*

RICHARD KATROVAS TELLS a unique story of how his own rootless childhood in the US led him eventually to have roots in two continents as the loving father of three daughters born in Czech Republic. Though he reminds the reader often of the unusual twists and turns of his early life—Dickensian barely describes it!—by the end of this book, he has, in fact, told the story of his generation, especially the men of his generation. The final essay, "Glenn Beck Is Not My Brother," is the best I know about the heartbreaking divisions in American society today.

    MARK JARMAN, author of *Bone Fires: New and Selected Poems*

IF, AS SOCRATES told us, the unexamined life is not worth living, Richard Katrovas demonstrates amply in *Raising Girls in Bohemia*, that a life considered rationally, and with sensitivity, reveals insight both triumphant and heartbreaking. This is a fascinating book. In these essays Katrovas proclaims unceasingly that the lives of his beloved daughters—indeed all of our lives—are not problems to be solved, but rather mysteries to be lived.

    GERALD COSTANZO, director, Carnegie Mellon University Press

AT ONCE DEEPLY personal and strikingly erudite, Richard Katrovas's *Raising Girls in Bohemia* is a remarkable achievement. In every piece the voice is authentically his, whether describing episodes from his exceptional life story, pondering the intricacies of fatherhood, or sidling into rumination on subjects as far-reaching as the role of art in society, the horrors of prison or the disparate ways we experience connection to past and homeland. This potentially random collection of essays is a true memoir and a satisfyingly thought-provoking read.

ELISE B. JORGENS, Provost Emerita, College of Charleston

SPEAKING FROM FIRST-HAND knowledge, I can say that Richard Katrovas is an exemplary parent, friend, and colleague, generous, tough-minded, invigoratingly opinionated, and tender hearted. As a writer of prose and poetry, he is simply an international treasure. All of these qualities are on display in *Raising Girls in Bohemia*, a wide-ranging collection of essays that speaks not only to fathers, daughters, and Bohemians both upper and lower case, but to all of us who matter to each other.

ARNOLD JOHNSTON, author of *The Witching Voice: A Novel from the Life of Robert Burns*

IN THESE TRENCHANT essays, Richard Katrovas strips away the gauzy romanticism of expatriate life to probe the challenges of raising three Czech-American daughters in a culture he *cannot* fully embrace—and that can never fully embrace him in return. In sweeping, meditative arcs, the essays roam from the author's own complex relationship with his incarcerated father to his struggles with the language and customs of Prague, turning always on the axis of his profound love for his daughters. A must read for anyone interested in the literature of expatriation.

ROBERT EVERSZ, author of *Gypsy Hearts*

A BRAVE MEDITATION on the hazards and fleeting forms of happiness available to a navigator of two divergent cultures. The American poet and prose writer Richard Katrovas explores the fallout from his doomed marriage to a Czech woman, and in the process addresses his own complicated inheritance—the ways in which his father's long-term imprisonment shaped his childhood; his fierce love for his three daughters and inability to protect them from heartbreak; the difficulty he finds in entering into another language and life. In these wide-ranging essays, Katrovas examines the nature of freedom, the artist's role in society, and the impossibility of ever really knowing someone, all with wit and wisdom. This is a wonderful collection.

CHRISTOPHER MERRILL, author of *The Tree of the Doves: Ceremony, Expedition, War*

Raising Girls
in Bohemia

MEDITATIONS OF AN AMERICAN FATHER

A MEMOIR IN ESSAYS

Richard Katrovas

WITH A FOREWORD BY PATRICIA HAMPL

THREE ROOMS PRESS
NEW YORK

ACKNOWLEDGMENTS:

Blackbird, "The Magic Book"
Callaloo, "My Transvestite"
Connotations, "Katie's Hair"
Crazyhorse, "Stalin's Face"
Ekleksographia, "School in Nature"
Fourth Genre, "The Lear Years"
Hunger Mountain, "The Underprivileged"
Mid-American Review, "A Brief History of My Heart"
Prague and the Czech Republic: True Stories, "Alan Levy 101: A Eulogy"
Solo Novo, "Glenn Beck Is Not My Brother"
Sonora Review, "Private Gold"
Southern Review, "Prison Art and Civic Pride" and "I Am Learning Czech"
St. Petersburg Review, "Poetry Is a Dead Art"
Third Coast, "The Big Easy and the Big Nasty"

Raising Girls in Bohemia: Meditations of an American Father
A memoir in essays by Richard Katrovas

Copyright © 2014 by Richard Katrovas

First printing

ISBN: 978-1-941110-06-5
Library of Congress Control Number: 2014938000

AUTHOR PHOTOS:
Annie Katrovas

COVER AND INTERIOR DESIGN:
KG Design International
www.katgeorges.com

DISTRIBUTED BY:
PGW/Perseus
www.pgw.com

Three Rooms Press
New York, NY
www.threeroomspress.com

This book is dedicated to
the mother of my daughters,
Dominika Winterová,
Queen of Bohemia

Contents

SPECIAL THANKS:

*I thank Stuart Dybek, Gail Wronsky,
Ema Katrovas, and Krista Katrovas for
reading and commenting on some of these essays.
I blow a huge, wet, weepy kiss of appreciation
to my friend and colleague Jaimy Gordon,
who, from the moment I met her, has been
the best teacher I've ever had.*

Raising Girls
in Bohemia

MEDITATIONS OF AN AMERICAN FATHER

Foreword

After 1989 and "The End of the Cold War" (which lately seems not so ended after all), Prague was the *it* city of Europe. A great city to be young in (or sort of young), to make—or especially to remake—yourself in. Prague became, as Richard Katrovas quotes an old journalist saying, "the Left Bank of the '90s."

Into this fevered redo of American expatriate dreams, Katrovas landed with his poetry and his ardor. He fell in love with a Czech woman and became a father, thus sealing his future as a man ricocheting between two worlds, past the marriage itself, but drilling ever deeper into the mysterious calling of being a father to girls.

These bracingly honest memoir-essays do not form, thank God, a trendy ex-pat tale. There is no fat of sentimentality about fatherhood to be burned away, either. Rather, the book offers a fierce encounter with oppositions, with American cultural domination and stubborn Czech certainties, with male and female powers and vulnerabilities.

The ground of the book is fatherhood and the contemplation of what it means to shelter girls, and launch them into an uncertain—make that a scary—but beautiful world. But the self-interrogation here is even more striking. It is a deeply moving, unstinting witness to an American boyhood and manhood (Katrovas's own), fraught with the desperate (and desperado) parenting he received from his con-artist father and his broken mother. For all its laser keen take on Czech life, the glory of this book is its reflected image of a hardscrabble American boyhood, cutting across the iron curtain of American economic class into the saving grace of independence of mind.

What is so amazing—the book is rinsed of self-righteousness, free of pieties. Its passions are never small or vindictive. From a harrowing childhood and an unsupported youth, there might be towering resentments on display. But these pieces refuse that cheap trick. A breakneck, wild determination is at work here. Honesty feels and sounds like this, going headlong into the past on a mission for the future.

The Czechs love the *feuilleton*, a literary form that is part personal vignette, part reflection, a form less stiff than the word "essay" suggests, and not as self-regarding as the contemporary American memoir can sometimes be. Richard Katrovas has claimed the form in these linked chapters, which build powerfully and exist with the freedom of mind that Montaigne, who wanted the *essai* to be an unfettered space for the mind, would surely recognize.

The title of the book is a wry irony—very Czech in fact—for it is not the girls who are raised in Bohemia, but the father and the American boy he was. A remarkable achievement, a heady ride, wise and knowing.

—Patricia Hampl

Introduction

I WAS TWO MONTHS AND FIVE days ahead of my thirty-seventh birthday when I held my oldest daughter Ema for the first time. I was twenty-six days past my forty-third birthday when I first held my second daughter Annie. I was fifty-one years, three months, and six days old when I watched my third daughter Ellie emerge from her mother's body. All three were born to the same Czech woman in the same sprawling, Dickensian, brick maternity factory in Prague 2, an enterprise whose bleak exterior belies its cozy interior. Though I wasn't allowed to be present at the first two births, I was admitted to the third because the strict prohibition of the father's presence in the birthing chambers had recently eased, yet another example of the Czechs' inexorable merging with the rest of Europe, and—by extension, though independently—with America, a process that over the past two decades has been by turns giddy and grudging.

I witnessed my third daughter issue from the body of a woman I knew I would soon divorce, a woman from whom I did not so much drift apart as beside whom I had drifted for fifteen years.

Our marriage was doomed from the start. My grotesque exit from my childless first marriage, the fact that my first daughter was the only reason I extricated myself from that union, and the psychic pressures of conducting a relationship on two continents, in two cultures, in the midst of child-rearing, rendered my second marriage untenable.

I'm told that in a good marriage, a real marriage, one's affection and respect for the other are primary, and one's love of children issues from that primary love. It's not that the love of children is secondary, but rather it is an extension, an augmentation.

My love for my daughters is fierce and direct, unmediated by, unconnected to, their mother, my feelings for her. She is a deeply decent, bright, and wise person, a beautiful soul and terrific mother, but I bound my life to hers for fifteen years only because I had children with her.

And my life is still bound to hers, though now that bond has no official name. To my heart, my ex-wife, Dominika, is Queen of Bohemia, a place in which I am but a resident tourist a few months each year. It is interesting now to note how the essays composed before our decision to divorce seem to predict the break.

In this book I explore the relationship between my own odd and unsettled childhood and that of my daughters. Further, I explore the effects of that relationship upon the way I see the world, how and what I value in this world at this stage of my life.

Most of these essays were composed over eight years, and in them I opine unashamedly on a range of topics about which I know little. The contours of one's ignorance may achieve a certain elegance, I can only hope, if one is not cagey regarding what he does and does not know or understand.

In midlife, following an eventful, sometimes even tempestuous youth, my focus has been on attending to the physical and psychological needs of female children. Throughout my daughters' lives, I have alternated primary parenting—that is, the traditional role of the mother—with their mother, and focused on them as intensely, though also, I hope, unobtrusively as a father may. Indeed, I have wondered from the beginning what the proper role of a father, especially a father of females in a postfeminist (in the same sense as "postmodern"), postmodern age, should be, and that question is a subtext of this book.

Of course, we have raised our daughters in the actual Bohemia of Central Europe, and the bohemia of American popular culture that now permeates even that ancient place after the fall of Communism. We also raised them, for a time, in America's bohemian capital, New Orleans. Whatever our girls become, however we may fail them from this point forward, they are now well-adjusted, worldly, bifurcated cultural beings who require and deserve a measure of privacy. I have shared many of these essays with my ex-wife and my oldest daughter, allowing them to vet what I have written about them. My ex-wife is not altogether comfortable with some of what I reveal in these essays, but does not contest any of my assertions and has not asked me to change anything, with the exception of misspelled Czech words, knowing full well that I would respect her wish that I change anything she finds truly offensive. Ema likewise has not asked me to change anything. Annie has been incredibly trusting and has given me permission to say what I will about her. Someday Ellie will read about her birth and how I felt about her in the months thereafter and know that though her conception was in the midst of some sadness, she was, immediately upon her arrival, a fount of joy to all.

I respect my children's maternal culture more deeply, as I finish this book, than I did when I began it. Though my ex-wife has asserted from the beginning that the Czech Republic should be their primary home, and I have countered that America should be, we both have come to realize that they themselves will decide where they are most at home, and that it is our duty, in our respective countries, our respective cultures, to make the best homes for them that we can as they are growing up, and then to conduct ourselves as gracious guests and hosts when we must visit one another's homes. But I now realize that the edgy tone of some of these essays, apart from being simply a reflection of my nature, has to do with the fact that my ex-wife and I have been engaged since Ema's birth in 1990 in a usually quite civil, even understated conflict as to which language and which culture will resonate most strongly in our children's hearts and minds. We have both feared losing our children to the other's culture. My ex-wife has feared losing them to the American behemoth and I have feared losing them to an extended family to which I cannot offer an American equivalent and to an ancient and beautiful place to which I could never, especially at this stage of life, assimilate.

So, I have been a reluctant, even at times grudging observer of Czech society, and that bad attitude does reverberate through some of these essays, but Bohemia has also served as a unique vantage point from which to regard my own bizarre childhood and youth, and from which to regard the culture that shaped my identity. Most importantly, it is my daughters' ancestral home, the one where their Americanness—their speaking English fluently and understanding American culture viscerally—will always afford them special status, whereas in America their Czechness registers hardly at all.

A BOOK SUCH AS THIS DOESN'T end; it stops. There is no obvious chronological point of resolution, except that five years ago my oldest turning eighteen, the portal onto womanhood, seemed a natural demarcation for such a project as this, an appropriate point to be silent about *her*, at least, given that from that age forward she was no longer a "girl" and I've not so much been raising her over the past few years as mentoring her, advocating for her. Her moral sense, her values, are set, and she is fast shaping a sophisticated worldview that jibes with some aspects of mine, some aspects of her mother's, but is wholly her own. Now, alas, only heartbreak, in its various forms, will finish the job.

I Am Learning Czech

CZECHS SHOULD DO AWAY WITH DIACRITICS, or maybe use them only sparingly like the French. It is a perfectly rational though unnecessary system invented by Jan Hus and enshrined by later academicians. Any non-Czech who has written about things Czech must face the decision to use those tricky little marks, or not, in place names and in the occasional italicized Czech word or phrase. No one but a Czech will know if they are correct, and they usually won't be. Still, including them is very cool; they make you look smart. I refuse to use them because I feel that they're pretentious when the person applying them doesn't speak, read, or write Czech. What Czech will read about things Czech in English, and so be offended by erroneous or missing diacritics?

I have been on Chapter Six for twelve years; that is, no matter which textbook I use, I can't get beyond *Lekce Sest* (little "v" over the first "s") no matter its content. In some texts, Chapter Six is quite advanced. In others, it takes one no farther than *To je hezka kniha*. But whatever its content, Chapter Six is my Rubicon; if I get past it, I'll be fully committed to a minimal competence that for reasons I can't fathom—something having to do with botched potty training or a cankerous character flaw too hideous to pluck at—I've been unable, or unwilling, to achieve.

In Chapter Six of *Communicative Czech* by Ivana Bednarova and Magdalena Pintarova (in Bednarova there are accents over both "a"s and a little "v" over the "r"; there is an accent over the second "a" in Pintarova), we meet Kristyna:

> *Jmenuju se Kristyna. Jsem z Bulharska. Ziju v Praze uz skoro mesic. Bydlim na koleji. Mam maly pokoj bez koupelny, ale jsem rada, ze bydlim sama. Kazdy den chodim do skoly a studuju cestinu. Skola je blizko krasneho parku.*

In copying this, I left out twenty diacritics, marks signifying that the *y* in her name is long, that three of the *"z"s* should be pronounced as soft *"g"s*, two of the *"s"s* like *"sh,"* one of the *"c"s* like *"ch"*, two of the *"e"s* rather like the *"y"* in "yellow." And, of course, in addition to her name, several words contain long vowels that should be marked by accents. She tells me her name is Kristyna. She is from someplace I'll assume, for now, is Bulgaria, because, of course, "Bulharska" is not listed in the glossary. She lives in Prague now almost a month, though I wonder if there is a way to say it in the present perfect that she's simply sparing me until, say, Chapter Eleven. She resides at a student dorm—probably Kajetanka, a wretched facility where many foreign students are stashed—in a small room that doesn't have a private toilet or shower, but even given this inconvenience she is happy because she lives alone, *sama*, more "by myself" than "alone"; it was Annie's favorite word when she was two and wanted to do everything *sama*. Everyday (*kazdy den*) Kristyna goes to school and studies Czech. The school is near a lovely park.

I can understand her being happy that she doesn't share her room with anyone, and accepting unfazed that she must share a toilet and shower probably with a dozen other young women. Czecho(slovakia) is much better off than Bulgaria, was much better off before 1989. The textbook was published in 1995, so Kristyna would be a decade older now, probably pushing thirty. I imagine that she met a nice Czech boy her third day in the country, and that her proficiency in Czech, as a consequence, improved rapidly, until he lied to her. Heartbroken, she sits an hour in that lovely little park near the school, that *krasneho parku*, and weeps, muttering curses in Bulgarian, which is a Slavic language and therefore quite close to Czech, though curses are unique in any language and are tender strings on the soul, strings that, plucked, sting sweetly. Dominika can curse in English like a landlocked sailor and think nothing of it, but when certain Czech curse words are uttered in certain contexts, she can be deeply and immediately affected. As Kristyna sits muttering curses in her mother tongue, tears welling in her eyes, she wishes she did not have to return to that cramped, cheesy dorm room in Kajetanka, where young men's body odor tinges the air, and where she cannot pee in private.

> *Vyucovani zacina v 8,30 a konci ve 12,45. Vcera jsem mela hezky den. Rano jsem vstavala jako obvykle v 6,30. Snidala jsem kavu a rohliky. V 8 hodin jsem sla do skoly. Psali jsme test a divali se na dokument "Praha-srdce Evropy."*

Her lessons begin at eight thirty and end at quarter to one, so I imagine she attended classes, then met him for lunch at the *kavarna* across the street from the school. He told her he couldn't take her to the family's *chata* over the weekend because his brother and sister-in-law would be using it, and, besides, his father is having heart surgery on Sunday so he, Petr, a student in the Philosophical Faculty of Charles University, must keep his mother and youngest sister company. When Kristyna asked why Petr's older brother and sister-in-law would be staying in the *chata*, and not in Prague to help Petr take care of his mother and sister during this family ordeal, his slow response was the classic befuddlement of a poor liar, and Kristyna knew immediately that Petr was getting back together with that horse's *prdelka* Olga, who'd stomped his heart innumerable times but obviously enjoyed the absolute control she exerted over his *ptak*: bird, which is one of the Czech euphemisms for penis, though surely Kristyna muttered its Bulgarian name.

Every school day I hear Dominika call, *"Vstavat,"* to the girls, telling them to get up, rise from bed. Kristyna rose from bed at 6:30 a.m. as she usually does, *jako obvykle.* But she is young and needs more sleep; surely she is irritable and tired, muttering and tearing up on that bench in the little park, where there is a sandbox and a bevy of young mothers and perhaps a *babička* or two, and small children squirming in the damp sand. This is not, not really, *"Den Kristyny,"* Kristyna's day, but I doubt that the phrase can resonate that way in Czech, as in, "This is just not my day." For breakfast she had only a roll and coffee, and her lunch had not arrived by the time she stormed out of the *kavarna*, so her stomach is growling and she's a little dizzy. No, this will not be a *hezky den,* a pretty day, or a nice day; it will be a lonely day, for after her fights with Petr her homesickness swells, and her head fills with the folk music her uncles used to pluck and scrape and squeeze from their horrible instruments at holidays, when she and her cousins romped around the groaning boards of their prolific mothers.

Now, in the middle of the first decade of the twenty-first century, Kristyna is thirtyish, wise to the ways of the world, wise especially to the lying ways of men; she lives with her Austrian lover in Naples, where he attends medical school and she is buying and selling cheap stuff on the Internet to make a decent living, but in 1995 she was too young to understand a fellow like Petr, a handsome, good-hearted kid but vacuous as a puppy, easy prey for that bitch Olga, who lived three years in Chicago so, now, in 1995, knows things. In less than a month Kristyna's romance with Petr has cycled through initial bliss to learning that he was on the rebound to learning that he was not at all over his previous girlfriend. They had one incredible week before the sour news of Olga, before the unraveling began.

Today, in 1995, after a test, she saw in school a documentary film titled *Prague: The Heart of Europe*. She smiles bitterly; she lost her heart in the heart of Europe. She is young enough to find the irony significant.

I don't want my Czech-American daughters to go through what I imagine Kristyna suffering, but how does a monolingual father help prepare daughters for heartbreak in two languages? Perhaps he begins by getting past Chapter Six.

Czech men, generally, are more decent than American men. They are chronically unfaithful, even more so than Americans, and I suppose in this they are not unlike most continental Europeans, especially the French. But they like women, seem able to form authentic friendships with women to a greater extent than can American males. There seem to be fewer gender pathologies in Czech culture generally, certainly fewer instances of violence. One advantage of my daughters hooking up eventually with Czech males will be that I won't have to talk with those young guys much. Unless my girls hook up with English-speaking Czechs, it is doubtful that the minimal Czech-language competence I aspire to will enable many soulful conversations with the young Czech guys my daughters present to me. The fact that I am large and look mean without trying will speak volumes, though.

If my girls connect with American men, I will unfortunately have to talk to those guys a lot. If they connect with white men from the suburbs, conservative types, I will weep privately but eventually buck up and try my best to be civil. If they connect with black men from the suburbs, I will be happy if those young guys are in medical school or are seeking some other postgraduate education. I'll do all I can to discourage my daughters from hooking up with working-class guys of any flavor who can't see beyond monthly paychecks, though I will embrace any males who love them and will not impede their progress toward whatever life goals my daughters set for themselves.

Regarding my teenager, Ema, I realize that these musings are near-future concerns, yet I'm not worried too much about her connecting with someone I won't like; I'm more worried simply that the first time her heart is broken she will be more deeply devastated than most young females, more susceptible to the transformative pain of heartbreak because she is more poised, tender, dreamy than most.

I don't want to imagine her teary on a park bench, devastated, homesick, cursing a young man by turns in Czech and English, feeling insufficient. My deepest wish regarding my daughters' hearts is that they never feel insufficient for being rejected in love.

And to this end I'll seek the proper distance each one requires of me, the proper degree of proximity, the appropriate degree of absence. I'll communicate in every way I can that until they fall in love with a task or idea, until they have wedded their fortunes to something larger than any man, father or lover, their hearts will be exposed to the vagaries of mere romance.

I met Dominika in the summer of 1989 on the Chatham College campus in the Squirrel Hill section of Pittsburgh, Pennsylvania. The Fulbright organization had decided I should learn some Serbo-Croatian before traveling to Ljubljana, Slovenia, where I would be a writer-in-residence at the university there; that the Slovenes considered Serbo-Croatian the language of their historical oppressors didn't seem to matter much. The Fulbright folks were willing to fork over a relatively hefty sum for me to study Serbo-Croatian in the Eastern and Central European Summer Language Institute on the Chatham campus, including meals, board, and travel, so I was game. I had no dog in the internecine conflict between the Serbs and the Slovenes, and arrived in Pittsburgh cheerfully ignorant of the languages, history, and politics of the region.

Dominika, a twenty-six-year-old who'd just finished her PhD in comparative linguistics and literature at Charles University's Philosophical Faculty, was brought over to teach the Czech course. The classes were five days a week, three hours a day, over six weeks. Most of the program participants were graduate students or faculty from good institutions, and many were scheduled, like myself, to hold Fulbright positions. A significant number arrived with some knowledge of the languages they were to study, or already had facility with a Slavic language. A perky young woman in my class of eight was fluent in Russian, and complained that Serbo-Croatian's similarity to Russian was sometimes confusing. She was chatting in Serbo-Croatian with the two instructors by the third week. One of my other classmates had spoken Macedonian as a child, and another had spoken Serbo-Croatian as a child; their

Slavic souls flooded back over the weeks and they, too, were conversing by the third or fourth week of the program. The others in my class were bilingual or multi-lingual, and though they had no Slavic languages they were tuned to the language-learning process. I'd been allowed to fulfill my college language requirements by taking a semester each of French, Spanish, Italian, and Latin so, of course, I knew very little of any of them.

I was the class idiot, especially given that I'd struck up a torrid affair with the gorgeous Czech instructor and was not conjugating and declining, except perhaps figuratively, deep into the nights, as were my classmates.

I was married, so I was cheating. I was indeed happily married, which is to say my wife was a good friend, so I was cheating not only in an institutional sense, which is almost meaningless, but fundamentally, which is to say my actions were a betrayal. I betrayed my best friend.

My first marriage was a joke. I mean literally. My first wife and I got married on a whim in New Orleans on St. Patrick's Day in 1980. We were drunk and stoned, and I cannot say precisely why we did it. I loved my first wife, in a manner of speaking, but more importantly I liked and respected her. She is decent, bright, and funny. She is beautiful, too.

As a young man, I was good-looking and must have had some kind of appeal, because I was intimate with numerous beautiful, truly beautiful, women. In fact, I have much more experience interacting with the psychologies of beautiful and attractive females than I do with the psychologies of females who are plain.

Beautiful women must learn to negotiate not only the attention of males, but also the envy and complex affections of women who are not beautiful. There are women who are comfortable with their beauty and those who are not; there are women, beautiful and not, who are comfortable with other women's beauty and those who are not. My first wife was comfortable with her own beauty and with the beauty of other women; perhaps more importantly she was a lover of women generally, which means that she sought and usually found the beauty in all women. Dominika is similarly democratic in her relations to other women. My first wife, Elizabeth, and Dominika share this advantage of being beautiful women in whom most other women, beautiful and not, sense this democratic impulse.

The value of Czech female beauty, considered as an indicator of national character, is best represented by the anecdote, perhaps apocryphal but saliently so, that in the midst of the Soviet invasion some young women would strike provocative poses in front of invading tanks then dash away. The purpose of this behavior was to set the horny young soldiers within ablaze. Allure used in such public service may seem poor fodder for martial ends, and yet it is quintessentially Czech, and illustrates both the matriarchal spirit of the culture and its indomitable passive-aggressive nature. Those daughters of Švejk hiking their skirts, dropping their straps, focusing come-hither gazes, were the frontline of a culture that had been defending itself against invaders for a thousand years by the only means available other than violent insurgency: irony.

The Czechs are the most ironic people on earth. A hundred thousand or more of them stood in Wenceslas Square giving the Nazi salute but singing their national anthem, "Where Is My Homeland?" Their history is rife with religious conflict, and yet theirs is the least faith-determined society anywhere. The national demeanor is a reversal of an old adage: "Light laughter on the face, deep sorrow in the heart." The Czechs do not guffaw, American and German style, in public; but there seems, despite deprivations and humiliations they have suffered, a well of hilarity at which all Czechs form a fire line, passing buckets. The conflagration of Czech history, including the charred corpses of Jan Hus and Jan Palach, smolders at the other end.

When my daughters' hearts are broken, will they despair in Czech or in English? Will they lock themselves away and listen to sad Czech songs or English? Will they place their faith in men such as I, and be cheated as I cheated the good woman I deserted to be with their mother?

They are the unmarred fruit of my deception. They are the blessings of my life, and though I have honored them I have been an asshole to their mother tongue, condescending to it, ignoring it, abusing it.

Kristyna fantasizes about confronting Olga, telling her to stop manipulating Petr; he is good and doesn't deserve what Olga is doing to him. Kristyna actually believes it is Olga's fault, that Olga is the whole problem. If it were not for her, Petr would see how good Kristyna is for him, how good-hearted she is, how caring. He would take her on the weekends to the *chata* in Slapy, and his family would treat her as one of its own; and that's really what Kristyna wants more than anything, to be a part of Petr's family, to feel part of a group bound by blood even though she is not related to it by blood, because it is the loneliness that makes her ache all over, the disconnection from familial intimacy. She spent one Sunday at the *chata* with Petr and everyone had been there, his mother and father, sister and brother, and brother's wife who had been particularly nice to Kristyna; Milena had treated Kristyna as a sister. They chatted for hours while scouring the forest floor for mushrooms, *houby*, and Kristyna had filled her basket with more than anyone as she had always done when her own family had hunted the fungi of her oldest uncle's woods, or the woods that belonged to him before the war.

At thirty, living abroad, Kristyna feels herself more European than Bulgarian; she speaks good Italian, fair English, and her best friend Olga, her former nemesis, jokes that she has become more Czech than Bulgarian, that her Czech is that good, and Olga's family, even her country-bumpkin cousins who live in the lower regions of the "Giant Mountains"—which are anything but—think of her as Olga's sister. Indeed, if her Austrian soon-to-be-doctor dumps her, as she realizes he likely will, it is to Olga and her family that Kristyna will retreat.

But now, on that bench in 1995, all she can think of is how terrible is that girl, *tahle holka*, that Olga she has only seen from afar, walking away from Petr's moped, or from his apartment in Prague 6, how manipulative, perhaps even evil, yes, evil. Petr is Olga's victim, and by extension so is Kristyna because she loves Petr, yes, she must now admit to herself on that bench, weeping quietly, hiding her face as best she can from the women on the benches around the sandbox twenty meters away, that she loves that boy, that kind, tender and funny boy, Petr Hašek, who once told her that he was indeed related to the great writer of the *Good Soldier Švejk*.

The patron saint of the Czech people is that ironic, bumbling soldier, whose moral lesson is subversive submission, which is to say his strategy is to submit to oppression then vex its agents with incompetence. Švejk and his progeny vexed three empires, but now are in danger of irrelevance as more or less unfettered markets render incompetence itself the oppressor.

My eight-year-old, Annie, and I went shopping one day last summer at the Tesco department store, whose proximity to

Národní divadlo, the National Theater, seems fortuitous given the latter's prominence in the Velvet Revolution and the former's role as a kind of center stage for post-1989 market relations. We sought a new pair of shoes for her, but didn't beeline to footwear, following rather a circuitous route, Annie dragging me through toys.

My second daughter is a tall, stunningly beautiful, blond, blue-eyed child; she is, in fact, beautiful like her mother and as willful as I. She's a good kid, but has a mean streak in which I secretly rejoice, for I know it will serve her well if I'm successful in training her to manage it, to be mean at appropriate moments without being mean-spirited, to have a nose for the kill but no malice. Because it's likely she'll be a beautiful woman, or even if she grows out of her beauty certainly no less a woman, she must learn not to be mystified by the brute strength of men, and to form strategies for counter-balancing the innate disadvantage of relative physical weakness. To this end, I don't bridle too much against her pushy nature, allowing her to delight often in overcoming my will, though asserting enough resistance from time to time to challenge and thereby strengthen her resolve. Sometimes I'm intransigent and her responses are fits of rage that are wonders to behold; her mother and I on those occasions gnash our teeth and wring our hands, but inwardly I feel triumph, for I know that person howling against the tethers of our authority will never be cowed, will never be oppressed, will never be struck more than once by a man she loves, Czech, American, or other. If I am a successful American father, there will be a strong consensus among those who cross her that she is a certifiable American Bitch, a type that is contrary to the Czech ideal of womanhood even more than it is to the American ideal of womanhood.

The Czechs have fashioned a matriarchal culture, and perhaps this is because they simply couldn't out-German the Austrians, or out-Russian the Russians, being themselves mostly failed Germans. Nineteenth century Czech nationalism was a matter of hauling a tiny Slavic dialect, one replete with so many diminutives Poles call it baby Polish, and its quaint folkish culture out of the mouths of Bohemian and Moravian grandmothers and into big-city opposition to German-language hegemony. Czech national identity wasn't an organic product of cultural accretion so much as an identity by committee; artists, statesmen, and intellectuals huddled, planned, divvied responsibilities, assigned duties.

But the folkish Czech heart is the same as every folkish heart; its deepest inclination is to hunker down, dodge conflict, tend the garden, avoid eye-contact with authority, though this feature is magnified in people with no martial past to glorify, whose martial past indeed is embodied by a beer-swilling fatso whose primary attribute, whose stellar quality, is incompetence. The Czech hearth is a place of primary power if only because it was never, to any significant extent, a place where women stoked home fires while menfolk battled Huns; it was rather almost always the place to which men stumbled bleary-eyed after long evenings of griping in pubs, the place to which they returned to be nurtured, cared for, attended to. Czech men generally don't oppress women by turning them into slaves, but by turning them into mothers, caretakers with all the responsibility but also all the authority. Czech culture, beneath the patriarchal veneer of nineteenth century nationalism, is a world of powerful mothers burdened by their interminable duties to prodigal, beer-pickled boys.

No American Bitch will put up with such a circumstance, for she won't have power on such terms. She asks only for a fair fight, a fair shot, a proverbial level playing field. The American Bitch is an advocate for gender fairness, and will recognize the paradox of Czech matriarchy for the dubious structure it is.

Communism accommodated Czech matriarchy fabulously; by driving private lives into the countryside, by flinging sex and fellowship, all things non-ideological, which is to say all things private and therefore humanly important, at the *chata*, the summer cottage, Communism simply reinforced, and deepened the paradox of, Czech matriarchy. Under Communism, women were installed in the workforce as never before, which meant simply that they were charged with maintaining the daily functioning of not only the workplace but both hearths, in the city flat and the country cottage. Men continued their Švejkish behavior unabated, remained coddled sons kvetching in pubs, shuffling from the care of women in the workplace into pubs, and then stumbling from pubs into the care of women at home, often with side-trips to their mistresses, who of course were themselves but doubly-surrogate mommies. So much of modern Czech literature, especially the novels of Kundera, is a clear, though seemingly unconscious, documentation of this circumstance.

So the Czech Mother, unlike the American Bitch, is classically conservative. She is in a traditional, if dubious, position of power; she is cheated on, condescended to, even slapped around from time to time, but she's in charge, whether she's checking out groceries or toys, serving food or flowers, administering pedicures or spooning cough medicine.

And I am constantly in conflict with these women in the Czech marketplace, especially given that I've been conditioned to receive service with a smile, to believe that I, the customer, am always right. I am infuriated when a cheerless country mouse acts as though she can't understand my tiny, grotesque Czech, tells me what a dolt I am in Czech she must know I will not comprehend unless she decelerates and mouths the words as to an addled one-year-old or genius dog.

Dominika, my beautiful and brilliant wife, sometimes wishes she'd married someone handy, a man's man who can fix things. I can see in her eyes sometimes that she wishes she could simply be a Czech Mother, run everything, and be exploited by a man who spends most of his time with other men in pubs and with a mistress (and so out of her way). Sometimes, I think, she is nostalgic for that life she could have had. However, instead, she is exploited by an American who would rather be at home than anywhere else, who does not seek the company of other men, but rather stays at home to read, write, and spend time with his children. She married an American who happily cedes all authority to her, especially when we are in Prague, an American who—though I cheerfully pull my domestic weight—is not only unhandy but militantly so. More often than not, she is happy to be my partner, particularly because I am a good father for our females and because I have been a good and faithful friend. She appreciates that I have trusted her implicitly, and passionately supported her career as a freelance interpreter. She realizes that our time in Prague is my time to read and write, though she wishes that I would not recede so deeply into myself when I read and write, when I work. Of course she wishes that I were not such an idiot regarding her language, but is beyond trying to shame me into learning Czech, for she knows that one of my meager, very American gifts is that I can't be shamed.

I think Dominika has weighed the pros and cons of having an unshamable American husband who in fifteen years has not learned her language. One advantage is privacy; she can talk on the phone to any Czech and know that I may get the gist of her conversation, but not many particulars. Another advantage is that our household is one in which our children must speak English and so our girls speak perfect Czech and English. A third advantage has been that over our fifteen years together her English has become spectacular, better than that of any of her colleagues.

Chief among the disadvantages has been simply that she must handle all significant transactions. I am not able to talk to my daughters' teachers, or to auto mechanics, or bank managers, or to the workmen she must hire to compensate for my militant unhandiness. She admires my work ethic, celebrates my career successes, but wishes that when we are in Prague I would not always collapse so deeply into my memories and imagination, cocooned in English; she wishes I would engage her world directly, open up to it and not filter it through her and our children. She wishes I could love her world as much as I love our children.

It is quite likely that Kristyna will never "find a man," will never marry. She is thirty and lovely, capable, resourceful. She wants children, and is even considering getting pregnant by her soon-to-be-doctor, though she has no delusions as to what would be his response to the news that she is pregnant. He would fly into one of his rages in which he abuses her verbally right up to the cusp of striking her; she has seen that sort of thing in men before. The American with whom she lived in Prague in the late nineties, an air force major and attaché at the US Embassy, raged once a week, struck her twice, though otherwise was gentle. The Czech men, too numerous to count quickly, had never struck her, had rarely raged, though they left her, always left her, and always for women that Kristyna knew, and former enemy, now best friend Olga insisted passionately, were not a fraction as beautiful and principled as Kristyna.

After a protracted scene in the toy section where Annie wore me down expertly and so acquired the object of her capricious affection, her shoes and toy now on the counter being rung up, I gave my AmEx card to the checkout woman who glanced at it and said in rapid Czech that it was no good because the black ink had rubbed off the numbers; I insisted that the black ink did not matter, that I'd never heard of such a problem. I had a Visa, but didn't wish to let that woman so arbitrarily, so ridiculously, determine the manner of my payment. I insisted, first in Czech (*This good. This very good. This not bad. What you say? Why you say this bad? You are very big idiot.*), but then noticed how embarrassed Annie was, not by the conflict but by how poorly I was conducting my end of it, so I explained in English that the card was perfectly fine, that black ink on the raised numbers had no bearing on the card's efficacy as an instrument of procurement. She smiled, fleetingly, the smile of a mother in charge, stood silent, passively fixed to her absurd position.

I wanted Annie to see me neither give in nor continue in my running role as American Asshole Abroad. A line was forming behind us; people's arms were full of stuff they wanted to place as soon as they could on the counter. The Czech Mother pinched my AmEx, stared at it. I reached over the counter and plucked it from her fingers, a provocative gesture in any culture. Then I slapped down my Visa. She processed it quickly. I signed and stormed away with my bag in one hand, the hand of my Czech-American beauty in the other.

Outside, I explained that the woman had been wrong, that she had been silly, but that sometimes, when we are right, insisting so is simply not worth the effort. The lesson was that we must learn to pick our righteous battles, and I went on to point out that by insisting upon my purchasing her bauble, Annie had spent influence capital, that I would not likely relent for her next fixation.

Of course she wasn't buying it. I watched her profile as I made my argument, threading through the crowd along *Národní třída*, amidst the Czech chatter which to her ears was a swirl of fully comprehensible conversations and to mine but a familiar babble of which I understood many words and almost no sentences, toward the tram stop where we would catch the 18 back to our home in Prague 4. I could see a kindred spirit shining from her eyes, the spirit of another being who like myself thrives on righteous conflict, my daughter, my bifurcated darling, my fellow American whom my American ex-wife, a good woman who chose to be childless for good reasons, would like and recognize as every inch my girl.

On that bench in 1995 a young woman, a girl becoming a woman in the crucible of heartbreak, is gathering courage to confront the cause of her sorrow, and she rises, rubs her wrists into her eyes, straightens her back, lifts her book bag to her shoulder, and strides out of the little park to search for Olga.

Prison Art and Civic Pride

When I was not quite eight years old, my mother confirmed what the kid downstairs had taunted me about. My father was indeed in prison. The kid's mother had noticed that the letters my mother received every day were from the federal facility in Harrisburg, Pennsylvania, and obviously had communicated this fact to the rest of her household. We were poor and white, on welfare; they were white working poor. Our family consisted of a woman and five kids of whom I was oldest, theirs of two parents and four kids. It was 1961. Our dilapidated, bifurcated rental in Elizabeth City, North Carolina, bordered the poorest black section of town just a few years before the end of (official) apartheid in America. We were the beginning of our black neighbors' containment.

I should have known my father was in prison. We were all together when he got caught, and the police had let me see him one last time in the holding cell before our mother took us on a Greyhound bus to Elizabeth City. He touched my face through the bars. But my mother had said it was all a mistake, that he'd gotten out and was now "learning a trade." We'd lived my entire life on the road while he scammed car dealers and wrote innumerable bad checks. That crumbling upstairs apartment was the first more or less permanent living space we kids had ever occupied.

For the duration of my childhood from the age of eight, I thought a lot about prison. It was a place, like heaven and like hell, that contained a father. It was a place from which voluminous correspondence issued. It was the origin of hope, because when our father got out of prison, life, we believed, would be better.

My entire adulthood I have thought a lot about prison, having avoided, barely, as a younger man, with the exception of a ten-hour visit to a holding tank, direct experience of such places. What I thought and felt as a child underpins what I now feel and think, though my childhood visceral connection to the idea of incarceration has broadened into an adult "interest." That is, I'm interested in the idea of freedom, particularly freedom of expression, and I'm interested in the actual physical relation of the artist to the state. Like almost everything else, this takes us back to Plato's rhetorical puppet, Socrates, who, even as he solved the problem of freedom of expression by insisting that the rhapsode have it elsewhere than in his, Socrates's, ideal community, was incarcerated and compelled to commit suicide for insisting upon it for himself. But across the ideological spectrum, the twentieth-century artist—Ezra Pound in his cage on the dock at Pisa, Aleksandr Solzhenitsyn in the gulag, Nâzim Hikmet in a Turkish prison, or Václav Havel in a Czechoslovak prison just months before becoming president —has focused, has stood as a synecdoche for, one of the fundamental philosophical issues of the age: what "freedom" means from culture to culture, political system to political system.

Over the past few years, four separate personal initiatives have not so much focused as refracted, like four lenses aligned at odd angles, this issue for me: opposing a prison arts project; teaching convicted criminals how to write poetry; "visiting" the site of the Nazis' "model" concentration camp; and considering the literary work of an American Gypsy-rights advocate. In each instance, my own motives were a muddle to me; that is, in each case I had strong feelings I could not wholly account for, feelings I knew were rooted in personal experience, but that I also knew were nourished by what I understand, alas too poorly, of the brutal history of the past century. In what follows I'm simply trying to find some clarity, trying to extricate complex personal feelings I may never fully understand from a sense of history that will never adequately account for what I feel. I'm trying to free what I know and feel about art and its relation to personal volition from a historical perspective warped by strong feelings that must be accounted for, even if never fully understood.

Until recently, I lived most of each year in the Czech Republic, in Prague, and the rest in New Orleans. With my Czech spouse I ran an arts and humanities summer program for a university in New Orleans, an institution with which I was affiliated for twenty years. I am a writer, probably best known as a poet. My spouse and I have two perfectly bilingual, bicultural Czech-American daughters, the older born—almost to the day—nine months after the demonstrable beginning of the Velvet Revolution, a glorious event I was privileged to witness on a Fulbright fellowship. This is all to say that I have been deeply invested in facilitating and encouraging all positive linkages between Prague and New Orleans.

A New Orleans lawyer who owns a bad-debt collection agency, a man of Czech descent who is the honorary consul of the Czech Republic in the city, recently worked a deal with Sheriff Charles Foti, the manager of the local jail. Foti's is one of the larger jails in the country, though New Orleans is quite far down the list of

US cities in population. When I took my kids to the "Christmas in the Oaks" celebration in City Park one year recently when we were in New Orleans for Christmas, we saw all the swell things the inhabitants of Foti's jail do for New Orleans children: they build wonderful life-size dollhouses, "Cajun Village" Christmas stuff kids love. It is delightfully unsettling to consider how such fanciful, even whimsical structures could have issued from the labor of men so far removed from innocence, and by this I do not mean to assume anything about their particular conflicts within the Louisiana legal system, but rather simply wish to highlight the dramatic contrast between their lives as incarcerated citizens and the nature of those structures they produce, under Foti's supervision, for children: stereotypical swamp shacks, draped in moss, decorated for a more or less traditional Christmas, and at night lit up gaudily for the "Christmas in the Oaks" processions of cars. As a father, I applaud such civic efforts, though as a fellow citizen of those prisoners, I do wish that Foti's name did not appear quite so prominently on plaques attached to those structures they, not he, labored to assemble. Saying this, I do not mean to chide Sheriff Foti, an elected official who has moved on to state-wide office, so much as to voice what many will no doubt consider a rather idiosyncratic prejudice: I do not like to see the names of politicians on public structures—buildings, bridges, or public works—of any kind.

The deal that the honorary consul made with Foti was for the latter's "prison artists" to reproduce as a mural a quite striking, tasteful, and lovely image fashioned by a colleague of mine in the fine arts department of my former university's Liberal Arts College. It's an image celebrating the connection between New Orleans and Prague, and the plan was to have the prison artists reproduce it as a large mural similar to the most recent one plastered over the jail's broad wall facing Interstate 10, a cartoonish memorial to Vietnam veterans. Under the helmeted heads of hound-dog-sad cartoon soldiers are words imploring rush hour traffic never to forget.

Though I celebrate the sentiment it embodied, I was repelled by that mural, assuming it unlikely that any of the guys who reproduced the image from God knows what source felt the sentiment they were reproducing, could possibly have cared if anyone traveling the main artery between New Orleans and points east remembered that people died in Vietnam, or could have cared that men still walk among us who were damaged by participation in that war. The demographics of Foti's prison suggest that his inmates—mostly between the ages of eighteen and thirty-five—are too young to have an emotional connection to Vietnam, and if you asked some of the youngest ones (and this is probably as true for the general population as for that of Foti's jail) if Vietnam is a country in Europe or Asia, they'd have to guess.

And so Foti's prison artists were to erect a symbol of the vital connections between Prague and New Orleans. That there are none (with the possible exception of my daughters) is beside the point. Oh, there are a few Czech-built streetcars rolling about, products of a Czech company recently under criminal investigation. And there is a student-exchange program at my former university that is quite vital and growing, but I'm not sure if those two "connections" warrant a mammoth mural. New Orleans is simply not brimming with Czech culture (even if there is a little enclave of folks of Czech descent in Libuse, Louisiana, a few miles to the southwest), though it is brimming with cultures

African/Creole, French, Irish, Italian, German, Hispanic, and, in fact, Vietnamese.

When I got wind of this enterprise, I wrote letters explaining why I found it offensive that prison labor would be used to produce "propaganda, even propaganda I agree with" (I was proud of that smug phrasing), and went on to pontificate about how *art, freedom*, and *prisoner* resonate as concepts in dramatically different ways, relative to one another, in Czech culture as compared to that of the United States, and that at the very least the project would appear highly ironic, even darkly comical, to many Czechs or to anyone with any knowledge of Czech history, for example anyone who may meditate upon Václav Havel, the Czechs' playwright president, as an inmate of a Communist prison just months before assuming his lofty position.

I was right, but for the wrong reasons. The fact of the matter is that I've never felt but the most fleeting interest in issues of prison reform and, though I thought the Vietnam mural rather silly (not for its sentiment but for the context of its presentation), never really cared about the thing longer than it took to swoosh by at seventy miles an hour. That the guys who paint Foti's murals get to hang out in the sunshine for a while outside that stinky jail is probably justification enough for the "prison arts" program. And the reproduction of benign propaganda is probably a more humane use of prison labor than the pouring and smoothing of pungent tar over miles of hot gravel. In the final analysis, Sheriff Foti should be praised for at least trying to create positive connections between the community and those of its members from whom he must keep it separated and protected.

In my self-righteous letters of protest, I was on solid ground opposing the mural, yet I was also in bad faith, at least a little, since my motives were anything but pure, because I'd not felt deeply enough the human circumstances behind my arguments.

I AM THE SON OF A man who spent half of my childhood in prison and the other half dragging his family all over the North American continent committing the crimes for which he would be incarcerated. I've written about my weird childhood elsewhere; suffice it to say that I have a complex emotional relation to the idea of forced confinement. I once got tossed in jail for a short while as a young man, and it was a horrible enough experience that I know, really know, that extended visits to such places should be avoided. I once, too, a few years later, visited the Angola prison near Baton Rouge, a maximum security facility with a reputation for being particularly rough. I was there to teach a poetry workshop, and though I'm sure there are folks who'll swear that such activities are wonderful vehicles for rehabilitation, and can testify to the healing power of poetry writing for such troubled souls as may attend prison workshops, I found the experience distasteful because this particular instance turned out to be much more about the liberal sentiments occasioning my visit than the actual lives of the men I presumed to lead through a process of "creative" expression. What they all needed was a basic grammar course, a basic history course, a course in how to solder pipe. If they needed to learn to express themselves better, such self-expression, practically speaking, should have been put, arguably, to a different end than art: each had failed to persuade some authority or authorities—a cop, district attorney, judge, jury—that his innocence was not a fiction.

On the occasion of my visit, they all acted sincere, and yet entombed in their phony sincerity was, it seemed obvious to me, an absolutely untouchable cynicism. I was just another liberal offering mild amusement and brief diversion from the nasty quotidian details of the hell they occupied. How did I know this? I'm the son of a con; appropriately or not, I saw my soul-sick father, the man who returned to us after his first stint in federal prison, in each of those men, those scam artists, those players of a system by turns exploitative, racist, inhumane, and yet determined as well by the liberal feel-good Second Chance ethos girding American idealism. That quality, that American Ideal, seemed a corpse each of those men was chained to, as it had been to my father. They dragged it everywhere, could never forget it, could never get the smell of it out of their heads, and could not but hold it in contempt. They wrote little ditties about stars and trees and Love and Freedom; they wrote the grossest clichés; none exhibited anything like talent; none seemed particularly smart. They all seemed patient, though, almost serenely, beatifically patient.

I did a great job, as did my two colleagues that day, another poet and a fiction writer. We were "honest" in our criticism, and yet, of course, tactful to a fault. We taught those sensitive cons about clichés and metaphor and point of view and abstraction. We taught them how to edit out superfluous adjectives and avoid passive-voice constructions. Then we got the hell out of there, couldn't wait to roll past the guard station and hit the open highway. I shivered for days thinking about shuffling through the various checkpoints to get to the "workshop," about the big-bellied guards, from whose girths dangled weapons, and who encircled the table where I and my colleagues enlightened those forgers, bank robbers, drug dealers, kidnappers, rapists, murderers, and every combination thereof.

In Terezín, for a time the Nazis' "show" camp—that is, the one they trotted the Red Cross through to trick world opinion—there is a permanent exhibition of the art of children, many of whom, soon after their creative interlude, were murdered by the Nazis, most of them in Auschwitz. I won't try to describe those images. Just imagine kids living in abject fear and privation, and imagine them with paper and colors. Then go there, or to the memorial at the Old Town Jewish Cemetery in Prague, and see those images for yourself. What is important, and grotesquely ironic in the context of this discussion, is that those images were in no way coerced or coaxed; they were images born of the free play of innocent imaginations. The day I "visited" Terezín, my group was led by a tiny man, thin and barely five feet tall, wearing a typically drab yet oddly colorful suit from the 1950s (the Czech fifties, not ours). He was drenched in silence, yet managed to say just enough at precisely the right moments; in other words, he was the perfect tour guide for such a simultaneously evil and holy place, and though he never said anything about himself, no one doubted that he spoke from experience, that he was a Holocaust survivor.

Near the end of the tour, he led all fifteen of us into a single cell, then spoke, slowly and calmly through the small opening in the cell door, informing us that exactly this many people had been forced to occupy such a cell, that people were smaller then, but that we should try to imagine fifteen people spending days in such a cell, working out a rotation system for occupying the single narrow bed, standing otherwise crushed together worse than on any subway car, for days. We were all writers; of course we imagined it, and imagined the smell, the sweltering heat, the stale air getting staler by the hour. And we imagined the horror of urinating, of relieving one's bowels under such circumstances. But to what end should such things be imagined?

There's an American, Paul Polansky, who's lived in Prague a number of years and has been active in the Gypsy-rights movement. His most enduring contribution to this noble cause has been an untiring commitment to the issue of the Lety concentration camp in southern Bohemia, a site where Czech monsters, enabled and emboldened by Nazi monsters ruling the "protectorate," gathered Gypsies and brutalized all and murdered many, even though most Gypsies were eventually transported from Lety to Auschwitz to be gassed. Lety is now a pig farm that the Czech government, inexplicably, will not remove and replace with a proper memorial, and the American Gypsy-rights advocate has bravely and with beautiful American stubbornness pressed the cause of a proper Lety memorial. He has also gathered testimonies of survivors of Lety, and published them in English translation with a small Prague press. The book is titled *Black Silence: The Lety Survivors Speak.* I attacked it in print not because the cause was not noble and humane, but because the book was horribly produced, amateurish in every aspect, and in fact the American author indulged in gross exaggerations and drew wildly irresponsible conclusions in his introduction to the Gypsy testimonies of their incarceration at Lety, oral narratives the author said he transcribed on a laptop from simultaneous Gypsy-language or Czech-language oral translations for which there are no verifying recordings. Polansky, alas, speaks neither Czech nor Gypsy.

I want a book of such testimonies of Lety survivors to exist, but one worthy of its subject. The poor editing struck me as hasty, ill thought out, and deeply disrespectful in the handling of a subject that touched so many lives and deaths.

What really confused and angered me, however, was that Polansky published, with the same small Czech press, with *en face* Czech translation, a book of his own poems, dramatic monologues in the voices of the survivors of Lety. That the poems were very bad is not the problem; what made me furious was that they existed at all, with no explicit or implicit apology for the sheer arrogance of their existence, that this well-meaning fellow, who'd locked on to a noble cause, had presumed to crawl inside the lives of people who'd suffered and to make "art" of their hell so unabashedly. If the interviews were valid records as he claimed, why was there a need to take those same voices and render them into texts substantially unchanged from the translated testimonies, but now broken into free-verse lines and "authored" by an American unable to speak either of the languages in which the victims had actually suffered?

MY FATHER IN FEDERAL PRISON PRIMARILY for forgery; young black men in Foti's jail primarily for breaking drug laws and being violent among themselves; cynical cons doing hard time in Angola; Jewish children in Terezín for being Jewish; Gypsies in Lety for being Gypsies. Some people get put away for what they do, some for what they are. Though there are those who would argue that the issue is always what you are. The difference between my stupid, white-trash father and a wily businessman is scope. The difference between a tobacco executive and a kid in Foti's jail, in most cases, is scope and race.

When we think about "art" and its relation to the artist, we usually think in terms of text and author, painting and painter; that is, we think of a singular ego in relation to the object of art. Of course, whatever postmodernism is, or was, it confounded the Romantic (and High Modernist) privileging of "artist," replacing author with "author function," etc. However, most of the "art" the world has known, indeed most art that has survived, has been the product of gigantic and largely anonymous public-works projects. St. Peter's Basilica contains Michelangelo's *Pietà* and his famous ceiling, but is itself also a work of art. Who would say that the Great Wall is not an aesthetic object? To know the name of the designer, the architect, of a massive building or monument is not the same thing as to know the name of the author of a book or the painter of a portrait. With rare exception, the designer of Big Art is always chained to the orthodoxy of whatever/whoever commissioned the project, and is then dependent upon the skill of the artisans and workers who actually bring the design to fruition. Whether commissioned by a religious tyrant, a Communist or Nazi butcher, or a reptilian captain of industry, Big Art, from the pyramids to the proposed National World War II Memorial in Washington, DC, is an advertisement for a particular worldview that has nothing to do with the dreams, terrors, and desires of the individuals who actually produce it, except perhaps in the sense that Big Art's monuments may enter dreams and be transmuted there into the stuff of Small Art. Big Art, in almost all cases, is communal and orthodox; Small Art is individual and potentially heterodox, though when it is, there may be consequences for the artist. The genius of Small Art—a poem, a novel, a painting, a statue, a sonata—is that it is tethered to individual volition; its subtext is always the relative freedom of its maker.

Much of what is grand and fixed, or simply large enough to be seen from a fair distance, through the ages, was produced by slaves and prisoners, or artisans and workers conforming to orthodoxy in response to the threat of enslavement or incarceration. Just in terms of simple truth value, what is the difference between a towering sculpture like the Stalin Monument in Prague, 1955–1962, touting the love and friendship between Czechs and the Russians who'd invade them in a few years, and a mural touting the love and friendship between Czechs and the citizens of an American city, most of whom could not find Prague on a map? What is the difference between an image produced by a doomed, incarcerated child unrestricted as to what she may create, and one produced by an adult who may be incarcerated by a police state for what she creates and disseminates? What is the difference between an artist who is free to express whatever he wishes without state interference but whose audience is profoundly distracted by sitcoms, video games, and the NFL, and an artist for whom an insistence upon just such freedom will lead to incarceration?

Most art is prison art, if William Blake's famous "mind-forg'd manacles" are taken seriously as endemic to the human condition. Any "serious" artist, any constant (in both senses of the word) maker of Small Art, is chained to compulsions and egocentric ambitions no less inescapably than the prison laborer or slave is chained to his Big Art task. Perhaps only when the work of art is conceived not as a commodity or monument or testimony, or prophecy or admonition, but as a gift, a simple gift, does the artist, the giver, achieve something we may call freedom, though the product of such freedom certainly will have no purchase on "greatness," "profundity," "wisdom"; such art (like most art) will certainly be ephemeral.

My father sent my mother a single gift from prison, for one of the seven Christmases he was behind bars during my childhood and adolescence. It was a handbag, a purse he said a buddy had taught him how to make. It was constructed entirely of Camel cigarette wrappers. He was probably lying; someone else may well have made it; he was never good with his hands. But it was exquisitely crafted, intricately and precisely woven so that hundreds of those kitschy camels faced in the same direction, and I'd like to think that he made it, that he saved his cigarette wrappers for months, years, and crafted for the mother of his children something in which she could hold and carry her small and necessary things.

The Underprivileged

I WAS CERTAIN, AS A YOUNG man, that socialism was the Answer, perhaps in the same untested sense that Right Wingers remain certain that Free Markets are the Answer. Both certainties are absurd, notwithstanding the most cogent arguments for either are perfectly rational.

I returned in the spring of 2004, with my family in tow, to the federal housing projects in Norfolk, Virginia, where I'd lived with my dying mother and four younger siblings from 1963 to 1966, from a few months after Kennedy's murder to the late summer of the year my father finished his second prison term. My Czech wife Dominika and my Czech-American daughters Ema, thirteen, and Annie, seven, were solicitous. They understood that the return was emotional for me, though I concealed my sadness with wry humor, jaunty chatter. We were on a ten-day road trip, through three states, financed by public readings I performed at several colleges and universities *en route*. Finished hawking my new book, I settled my family into a high-rise hotel on the Virginia Beach strip, just a few miles from a home, a cramped cinder block and brick apartment, I'd not looked upon in thirty-eight years.

Nothing had changed on the main boulevard leading to the projects, at least nothing that could be judged an improvement. Before entering the projects, we parked along the Elizabeth River, across the street from the house of four girls I used to visit, auburn-haired sisters ranging in age from sixteen to six. Margaret Mason, the third daughter, was in my grade and liked me; I originally visited just her, but became a family pet, and Margaret's older sister, Charlene, was the first girl I ever kissed. The sixteen-year-old, Mary Anne, was the one I really wanted, though I was eleven and then twelve, and didn't know—well, I knew but not *precisely*—what that attraction meant; she showered me with smiles, loved to talk to me, would iron a skirt and chatter to me about high school stuff, and I'd hold my knees before her, sipping Kool-Aid, gazing up adoringly, inhaling her smell over the steamy starch and artificial cherry flavor.

They were rich people, kind of. Their large white house had changed little except that it was shabby, as were now all the houses on that street where no development had taken place, absolutely none, where even the meager trees on the riverbank had not changed except to seem unkempt, where the stunted thorn tree in which I'd pierced my skull an eighth of an inch deep still drooped in haggard defiance of my expectations; where it seemed the same bald tires tilted half buried in the oily sand, and the same debris, bread wrappers and gull feathers and condoms, wreathed the river rocks.

The Masons knew I lived in the projects three blocks away, but didn't seem to make much of it. I didn't tell them my father was in prison, that we were on welfare, though certainly my dress and manner didn't suggest otherwise, or suggested only that I was poor, kind of. Even then I knew that, from a global perspective, "poor" is relative: several months before the FBI caught my father, he'd driven us through Mexico. In the projects, my mother, siblings, and I weren't destitute, just underprivileged, which is to say, I suppose, that we suffered from a privilege deficiency; we required, the body politic owed us, more privilege. But relative to what? To whom? The Masons?

The projects were segregated: black on the south side, white on the north. We occupied the very last apartment in the very last unit at the white end of the projects, a bifurcated brick community of two-story structures, each unit containing six to ten apartments, which sprawled in groups of three for over half a mile. We butted up against a lower middle-class neighborhood of mostly black homeowners. Now, those projects are all black, as are the surrounding neighborhoods, including that one along the Elizabeth River into which I'd interpolate myself to stare longingly at Mary Anne Mason.

I don't recall a single racist remark by anyone, white or black, in that extended community of segregated housing projects and surrounding black and white patchwork neighborhoods, and I find it miraculous that I don't. But I don't recall "racial tension" at all, only moments of wariness that quickly withered. My school, Margaret's and my school, Chesterfield Heights Elementary, was predominantly black, only integrated two or three years previously. We all got along, though I'm not really sure why or how.

I wonder if it wasn't because we were in the midst of a revolution, the Civil Rights Movement. Perhaps we all felt invested somehow in those changes, through our common participation in, our materially benefiting from, the Great Society, even though we really didn't know anything about those changes *qua* changes, at least we kids didn't because we had no point of comparison. In the projects we were, black and white, underprivileged, and I assumed, of course wrongly, that we were pretty much equally so.

I don't know what the adults thought or felt, especially my mother, who was dying of multiple sclerosis. She was mostly in despair, and when she wasn't she didn't spend much time musing over social issues, at least not aloud. She was a beautiful young woman with a quick wit and dreamy nature who, inexplicably, allowed a crazy and handsome young man to drive her, without destination, across America for seven years, impregnating her numerous times along the way.

I left Dominika and the girls in the car and walked up to the door of that apartment at the end of the projects, at the end of that world, and stood on the narrow slab of concrete before the entrance to my old home. I did predictable, stupid things like touch the bricks, the wood, the rusted number, ran my fingers along the windowsill to the right of the door. If I knocked, and someone answered, what would I say? Hello, I used to live here. May I see my mother's room? May I sit at the kitchen table and look around? May I use your toilet for nostalgia's sake? May I peek under the kitchen sink? May I curl up in the dark of the tiny pantry behind the fridge? Does it still smell of rotten potatoes? When you snap on the kitchen light, do the roaches that have scurried through the flour still look like ghosts, or Caucasians, among the ones that haven't yet?

The child faces of my siblings grew vivid: Chuck, Terry, Art, and Chris, whom I took care of and brutalized a little, to whom I'd return late afternoons in summer after hours of roaming the neighborhoods seeking thrills and all manner of sustenance: working in yards for quarters and stealing fruit from trees.

Moving through those rooms, would I hear their whimpers, their laughter, their screeches by turns forlorn and ecstatic? Would I smell the sour spunk of unwashed children and laundry?

Would there be a TV whose rabbit ears were augmented at the tips with crinkled foil? Would it have been broken for months, dormant before the battered couch? Would all the beds be urine-stained? Would there be a box in a closet filled with letters from someone doing hard time?

In America, the dance of Nostalgia with Upward Mobility is an ugly polka, something a little silly, but tenderly so. I stood frozen before the door of early adolescence, roiling in sentimentality I didn't try to thwart, assuming I'd earned that particular moment by waiting so long to feel it. My heart is no more pure than my politics, is at least that muddled, confused, but for the clarity of overwhelming moments when the pain of others humbles.

On such thresholds, the music of the spheres is audible, and it is the sound of rushing blood, that mid-life tinnitus that distracts from the terrors of silence. Ema asked why I hadn't knocked. As I started up the Camry, two white cops strode from an apartment unit a hundred yards away. I scanned the street, where I'd witnessed a retarded white kid bleed to death after he'd been struck and dragged by a Studebaker as he'd tried to fetch a ball; where, black and white, we'd raced popsicle sticks in gutters after hard spring rains or chased the singing ice cream truck; where few cars parked because few residents, black or white, owned them, and where I ran at dusk on errands, familial missions, to buy my mother's packs of Pall Malls for a quarter apiece at Comstock's, a can or two of beans-and-bacon Campbell's soup for less. It was a socialist community, not unlike the ones I'd stroll through in

1989 in the months leading up to the Velvet Revolution in Prague, Czechoslovakia, except that the housing projects outside of Prague were massive, degenerate high rises whose tiny, cluttered flats were as likely to be homes to engineers, professors, and middle-managers as to those merely languishing on the dole.

Capitalism fails the weak, socialism the strong. Neither, in anything like its pure form, works for long. And yet there can be something like a socialist heart and a capitalist heart, one that is comfortable with egalitarian intimacies and a spirit of sharing, and one that is acquisitive and seeks superiority for its own sake. How often do we encounter hearts that are purely one or the other?

On the days the checks arrived from welfare, one hundred and sixty-nine dollars for that month, of which sixty paid rent, we'd have a kind of celebration. My mother would cook something especially good, even after her illness grew grave. She'd support her weight by pressing down on the counters of the tiny kitchen, lean her braces against the stove. The back door to that kitchen opened onto a patch of dirt stuck with a circular clothesline; each apartment in the horseshoe of units had a patch of dirt, and some were tufted with weeds and grass, some not, and each little square was stuck with an aluminum pole. The patches were fenced with chain-link, three feet high, and when I caught the odor of special food wafting through the tattered screen, I could jump over that fence, take a running start, leap, lift my knees to my chin, and float, as though in the palm of Adam Smith's invisible hand, from the common ground to our patch, our yard.

My Transvestite

SOMETIMES ANNIE, MY SECOND DAUGHTER, INSISTS upon making me over. Most fathers of girls know the drill: Garish tattoos, composed with multi-colored ballpoints, covering both of my arms; enough mousse to give my hair the tensile strength of bungee cord; and, on those occasions she simply saps my will with her relentless intent, make-up. When she is finished, everyone must laugh at me, pitilessly, for, as anyone who knows me will testify, I would make a very unattractive woman.

My daughters, especially the teenager, intuit that gender identity is at least partially a construction, as much nurture as nature, though it is intuition tutored by experience, specifically the years we lived between New Orleans and Prague, as now we live between Kalamazoo, Michigan, and Prague, with forays down to the Big Nasty as often as we can manage. My girls have grown up assuming drag queens are as natural a feature of the urban landscape, at least in New Orleans, as stumbling tourists tangled up in gaudy plastic beads and sloshing Hurricanes from go-cups. Both will speculate matter-of-factly as to whether this or that fellow is gay, and both notice the cultural difference between New Orleans and everywhere else, though particularly Prague, regarding gender identity as street theater. We've never seen a transvestite in Prague, at least that we've been aware of, never passed a rollicking gay bar. The gay life in Prague is discreet to a fault. The transvestite community is either non-existent or so discreet as to be meaningless: What transvestite can feel fulfilled living discreetly, at least up to a certain age?

I wonder if the flaunting of contrary gender isn't a celebration of one's power to choose from the midst of that most fundamental aspect of identity that cannot be chosen, except in terms of "reassignment." I mean, those transvestites who believe themselves women trapped in men's bodies choose to be what they ostensibly are not, and what more radical gesture of freedom can there be than that? It isn't a lie, but a paradox: I am a male, but I am a female.

Such radical freedom requires a haven; New Orleans, before Katrina, served as such for several decades, and one can only hope that it will remain a charmed urban space where men and woman who have been marginalized to the point of endangerment across the American South come to form a center, a play space where one of the most powerful transformations imaginable may be afforded its existential due. I have had the privilege to know the embodiment of such freedom, its corporeal and spiritual essence, though I was too distracted at the time to appreciate her.

She was a grim parody of femininity, a humorless, white, petite biological male with big eighties hair and olive skin. She was large-featured, exotic, but not very pretty. She hardly ever wore dresses, usually entered the classroom in tight slacks and pastel blouses unbuttoned and knotted at the ribs. Her make-up was tasteful, usually.

It should surprise no one that in New Orleans the range of students I encountered at the public university where I worked for twenty years reflected, in every significant respect, the demographics of the city. I taught scores of "Y'ats" (white, upper Ninth Ward natives named for the salutation, "Where y'at!"); Chalmette natives, always white, called "Chalmatians" (about whom a young knucklehead from Jefferson Parish might joke: How do you compliment a Chalmatian on the first date? You tell her, "Nice tooth!"); black kids from all over predominantly black Orleans Parish who chose to attend my white-flight public university rather than the city's mainly black public university for complex, often noble reasons; white students from Metairie, the Irish Channel, Algiers, even Slidell, in all the ethnic flavors, though mostly Italian and Irish, mostly Catholic. Of course, I worked with numerous "ESL," English as a Second Language, students, from Vietnamese to Salvadorian. I even taught some rich, white, uptown empty nesters returning to school to improve themselves, slumming at the local public institution. But this diversity extended beyond ethnicity, race, class, and religion to include sexuality and gender identity.

There are significant lesbian and gay communities embedded in every major American city and most minor ones, and that's as true for the South as for other regions of the country. New Orleans for a long time sustained one of the more vibrant populations of gay men and lesbians anywhere in the world, and most of them I'm certain are indeed Southern, "homo grown" as a lesbian friend once quipped, because the genius of the city, from within, seems as much Southern Camp as Cajun Cooking and Dixieland Jazz.

And what is Southern Camp? It's a lot of things I've little right, as a straight male, to expound upon, but it is, besides so much else—and I'm excluding here for brevity's sake its lesbian aspect—when a gay Southern man of a certain age gets a little drunk and starts acting, often quite unconsciously, just like the black woman who raised him in Selma, Mobile, Oxford, or Baton Rouge. It's the way so many Southern gay men, black and white, idolize black Southern women, black gay men the mothers, grandmothers, sisters, and aunts who raised them, white gay men the domestic help, the maids and childcare givers who were their first strong female role models. Through the seventies and early eighties, when the boys, white and black, were in full bloom in Lafitte in Exile, it wasn't, usually, the stereotype of a prim Southern belle they were emulating, but that of an earthy woman of color out on the town.

Any given semester, I'd have several gay and lesbian students in my poetry writing workshop. They were usually a little older than the other students, often close to my own age or even older, and the gay men, as *Southern* gay men, were often not only purveyors of Southern Camp, but, like the Southern black women many adored, tended to be emotionally, as well as physically, tough. Not too many gay Southern men (or women, for that matter) of my generation made it out of childhood and adolescence without a fight, and it was often the black women, in the males' lives anyway, who showed them how to stand up for themselves. And of course every gay person was a survivor, was in certain respects like the Vietnam vets I sat next to in classes in the early seventies, wiser for the devastation and losses they had so recently experienced, and ruing that wisdom. All of them, every single one I can remember, had cared for dying men, the lovers and friends of their youth.

I'm on dangerous ground, of course, dealing in stereotypes, even caricatures, but if living in pre-Katrina New Orleans taught me anything it was the paradox of caricature, how it cuts both ways, demeaning and celebrating. The essence of Mardi Gras as well as of Southern Camp, the relationship of the two being complex and mutually determining, is celebratory caricature.

My transvestite student was a little nuts, even though her being so I was certain had little or nothing to do with her gender identity, and though that identity seemed to soak more deeply into her consciousness than the intrinsic ironies, the social genius, of camp; she was an unsophisticated person in her early twenties, poorly read, sadly disconnected, as far as I could tell, from any community of transvestites in a city known for its grand extended communities of such folks. Her isolation was not a cause but a symptom, I assumed, of a psychological malady I wasn't, and still am not, qualified to identify and respond to appropriately. "A little nuts" is hardly the phrasing a professional psychologist would use, but I'm not a psychologist, and the skill to recognize students' psychopathologies was never mentioned in any of my university job descriptions.

In what sense was my young transvestite—let's call her Rosy—a little nuts? She spoke in *non sequiturs* that were not, at first flush, reminiscent of Lear's fool; they were juvenile and troubling, interminable and distracting. The gay and lesbian students in the class were the most critical of her behavior, the most troubled by the fact that she seemed, well, a little nuts. I, of course, try not to enter into any sort of conspiratorial conversation with students regarding their peers or mine, but when two of my transvestite's colleagues—hip, very adult women—came to me to complain that Rosy was a powerful distraction in class, I asked them, assuming that they understood social marginalization, as lesbians, better than I did as a white, heterosexual male (and prefaced my query by voicing that assumption), what they thought I should do.

After chastising me for my politically-correct stereotyping of them as "marginalized," one, quite wisely, pointed out that Rosy's problem, her distracting behavior, her babbling for minutes about nothing connected, at least in any obvious sense, to the topic at hand, was probably the result of some sort of chemical imbalance. In short, Rosy reminded her of someone who'd stopped taking her meds. I'd been viewing Rosy's presence in fairly simplistic social/political terms, when I should have been regarding her in terms of her (obvious?) need for mental health care.

To this day I don't know how Rosy even got admitted to that university. I have my suspicion that she was admitted as a "special" case, similar to another student a few years previously who'd called me several times after midnight threatening my life. I only found out after a week of having university police stationed at my classroom door that that chemically imbalanced person had been admitted to my class as a form of "therapy" prescribed by a psychiatrist; my chair had arranged his placement in my class, but because of confidentiality laws couldn't inform me of the circumstance. The poor fellow's schizophrenia reemerged when, alas, he stopped taking his meds.

Rosy lurked, literally, in shadows and around corners and in doorways, not to do harm, but simply, it seemed, to appear suddenly, to enter one's field of vision full-blown. I recall turning a corner once and coming face to face with her stare; it was as if she'd been waiting. She didn't smile, made no expression at all, just stared directly into my eyes, her eyes straining to be as wide open as they could be. Hello, Rosy, I'm sure I said, and probably tried, after gathering myself, to make small talk of some sort, but Rosy wasn't able to talk about anything small; she seemed always to be swinging for the metaphysical fence. She said something like, Why do you hate my poems? Why don't you see that I'm a genius? Do you hate me because I don't have a vagina?

I tried mightily to persuade Rosy, on several occasions, that I did not hate her, for any reason, that I didn't hate her poems, I just thought they "lacked focus." What I didn't say was that her poems weren't good enough to hate, that a profound naïveté shielded her from my loathing, a naïveté that seemed the aura of irrepressible madness.

In class, if the topic at hand were William Carlos Williams's idea of the "variable foot," or one of Empson's *Seven Types of Ambiguity* as it seemed to apply to a student's poem about her dead mother, Rosy would break in quite suddenly after forty minutes of being conspicuously silent, and, apropos of absolutely nothing that wasn't churning exclusively in her own brain, begin babbling about her "ghost period," how every month she felt all the symptoms of menstruation without actually shedding blood, about how as a child she would stuff her mother's Kotex in her drawers and spend the day complaining of cramps, how a woman's place is in the home making babies and cooking for her man, but that babies someday soon will grow in glass beakers, and thus will wombs be rendered obsolete. Oddly, some of what she said might arguably be connected, for example, to the fact that Williams had been a pediatrician, and maybe one of the other students would have made a breezy reference to the good doctor's "To a Young Housewife," but such connections remained, in this case, sadly unexplored.

What are the protocols for such a circumstance? Her texts, by my fairly conservative aesthetic criteria, were an incoherent jumble, but even those in the class who found her tirades most distracting, most troubling, were often willing to advocate for such writing, take it on its own postmodern, non-referential terms. One of the brighter members of the group even said that Rosy's best poems reminded her of Jorie Graham's work, though such a comparison was pure mischief. However, if Rosy was producing, on time, sufficient and—by the reigning standards of the day—appropriate work, and if indeed she would usually stop talking her nonsense when asked, what was my professional responsibility?

And what if that nonsense she spoke was only a little more coherent, more interesting even, than the nonsense she wrote? Why should I insist that the discourse of the classroom be fundamentally different from that of the *subjects* of that discourse? What's the difference between some of Charles Bernstein's poems and his statements of poetics? Nothing. They're often the same text, as was true of Alexander Pope's texts. Besides, if irrationality and "non-referential" fields of language can constitute art, why can't they constitute the discourse *on* art? If a student chooses to "speak" art in response to art, do I have the right, the responsibility, to censor her?

I'm talking about a kid who probably stopped taking her meds, or should have been taking them but was never prescribed any. But I was engaging her in a poetry writing workshop, a location where not only should a thousand flowers bloom, no matter how exotic or hideously mutated, but where it was my responsibility to protect them. If Rosy had written straightforward texts in which grisly murders were described, or in which children were victimized, it would have been much easier to justify taking those texts to my chair and trying to begin some process by which Rosy's problems would be addressed. But what would an English department chair, a scholar of some flavor of nineteenth century novel, for example, or a specialist in composition pedagogy, make of Rosy's poems? He or she would have probably thought those texts didn't look much different from the incomprehensible drivel she came across thumbing through many slick literary magazines. They'd have hardly represented sufficient evidence of debilitating craziness to justify taking Rosy out of the class if she was otherwise meeting the course's criteria by being physically present, turning in pages with words on them, and speaking up in class. Of course, if I'd required a formal critical paper, a personal essay, even, for that course I'd have had no trouble using Rosy's performance as evidence for evicting her, but, alas, for that particular class I hadn't stipulated such a requirement.

When Rosy turned up at my door during office hours I tried not to cringe. She would sit silently for a long time, placid, staring. I would fill the silence with teacher chatter, pausing as often as I could to allow her entry to a conversation, but she would simply continue to stare, practically without blinking, directly into my eyes. I'd ask her why she'd come, and she'd mumble that she needed help. I'd ask what kind of help, help with what. She'd thrust, seemingly from nowhere, a crinkled page at my face. I'd take it and read. It would be covered with the same words in the exact same pattern as the poem she'd turned in the previous evening to be critiqued by the group. She'd ask then why I didn't see that she spoke for Jesus, who was herself a woman trapped in a man's body. I'd weakly respond that I simply didn't see how that particular text could be a dramatic monologue. She'd say that Mary knew Jesus was a girl, dressed her up like one all through childhood, but that in Heaven there are no vaginas, that angels have absolutely nothing between their legs, and I'd have to say, well, Rosy, I think someone else is waiting in the hall; really, Rosy, you'll have to leave now.

I never saw her smile, much less laugh. On good nights, I'd have my students rolling in the aisles, well, chuckling in their seats, anyway, and Rosy would be inscrutable, staring in that wide-eyed creepy way. I had never known a flaming queen with absolutely no sense of humor, never known such an individual not plugged into camp consciousness, even its bitter and nasty, bitchy versions. She spoke with a Mississippi or Georgia accent, I can't recall which, intoned more like a Southern Belle than a Southern woman of color, and though she was tenacious, there was no fight in her. She apparently cared that I didn't affirm her genius, but seemed to view this as my failure of the other students and myself, not so much of her.

Across the street from my apartment in the French Quarter, where I lived for several years, at the height of the AIDS plague's first wave, on St. Louis between Bourbon and Dauphine, two doors down from Al Hirt's townhouse, the drag queens sashayed from midnight to dawn in and out of the Roundup, one of the cheesiest, nastiest establishments in the Quarter. So many pre-dawns I was awakened by brawls and other plays of passion, one drag queen screeching her sissy ire for a bad dope deal as she pounded her associate into the curb, or a butch tourist from Kansas wailing the name of someone he wanted desperately to believe was a woman. I learned to sleep through such theater, or past it, but it entered, often, my last dreams, the potent ones before waking, dreams in which people did terrible things to one another then wept remorse, or in which happy demons sang praises to the moon. There are those among us we may only in good faith know in the theater of such dreams, who will dazzle and instruct us from that proscenium on which truth is declaimed in riddles.

It is there that our most important teachers appear to us disguised as fools and madmen, as terrible infants and old indigents with crumbling minds. Those with the courage to lean upon the sharp edges of life, who *other* themselves because they have no choice or because to choose otherwise would be the death of joy or of its merest possibility, lead us, our bloody sockets bandaged, to chalky cliffs, to the sound of distant crashing waves, and there they trick us into living.

Rosy stopped attending class; I heard that she'd gotten in trouble for insisting upon using the women's room in the library, and since she insisted upon using the women's room everywhere else—my other female students mentioned in passing that at the breaks she'd join them in the one nearest our classroom—I wondered why in the library it would have been a particular problem. Obviously, someone there had taken strong umbrage, maybe a nice girl from Chalmette who'd had to do the peepee dance in front of the stall until Rosy emerged, flipped her hair, and sauntered to the mirror to fix her lipstick; or, more likely, a closet-queen assistant librarian who watched Rosy enter the women's room and was diminished by her nerve.

But it wasn't nerve; it was destiny steering that delicate yet tenacious soul into the contrary rooms, around corners neither forbidden nor forbidding, to lurk with no malice, with only the need to show, show everyone, that she was there.

Private Gold

"Fuck" is what you say as your 747 spirals down, or when a saucy ravioli falls off your fork onto your sleeve. No one says, "Oh, pussy, I forgot my keys!" Fuck is an instance where signifier and signified are often nowhere in sight of one another. Fuck is on the same order as God; in fact, they're often interchangeable: "Oh, God, I can't believe this is happening." "Oh, fuck, I can't believe . . ." But "pussy" is singular, except in the context where it means a guy who lacks courage, suggesting that he is like a female. I recently witnessed my third daughter's birth. In the Czech Republic, only in the past few years have they encouraged fathers to be in the delivery room, so I missed seeing the births of my first two girls. Having witnessed my third baby's birth, however, I must say that it is incredibly stupid that pussy, in its public usage, ever signifies anything that is not the very essence of courage and fortitude.

Every male, straight and gay, on his sixteenth birthday, should be required to sit behind a one-way mirror and observe a birth. Not just the climax, but the several hours of contractions preceding the money shot, and then the aftermath, the placenta being dragged out and examined, the sewing up, the cleansing of the whole bloody mess. If I'd been compelled as a boy-man to witness a birth, my life would have been changed for the better, I think; it wouldn't have taken me so long to realize the power of pussy, that that power has nothing to do with allure, which is incidental. Its power has to do with its being the portal onto life. That I abstract "it" from the whole woman here duplicates sexist objectification, but I think that such objectification is pernicious only outside the context of specific intimacies and thoughtful discussions. "Dirty words," indeed, may season the private talk of erotic intimacy regardless of gender configuration.

The distinction may seem simplistic, but I think it's profound. To the extent that female genitalia become a synecdoche for womanhood, as in pornography and locker-room talk, male authority is reinforced, and pussy then is merely that which accommodates male lust. But when the emphasis is upon, not accommodation of the penis, but, rather, the introduction of life into the world, an event to which males are marginal (as in standing by the bed useless but brimming with good will as the female writhes in agony), the shift in regard cannot be more dramatic.

So why bandy the word at all, why not simply acknowledge that it is sexist and meant to reduce females to their genitalia in the most demeaning sense? Because keeping pussy in the Ghetto of Dirty Word, allowing it to maintain its status as filthiest of filthy nouns, only strengthens its power to offend and therefore demean. One of the great linguistic coups in recent years was the gay community's appropriation of "queer" from the homophobic lexicon, reversing its charge from negative to positive. And the African-American idiom that forbids non-African Americans from uttering that most wretched of designations, even as the progeny of the victims of what that word embodies bandy it relentlessly, flaunt it publicly, is a stroke of genius that must be unparalleled in the annals of argot. Not just the second but both instances, of course, carry implicit prohibitions; heterosexuals may not with impunity call homosexuals queer just as no white person may with impunity call a person of color nigger. Similarly, I think that pussy should be embraced rather than prohibited, reconfigured to represent not the object of lust, but the source of life; and any woman who then tells me that *she*, but not I, may bandy the word will receive my whole-hearted assent.

My only caveat would be to point out that sexual epithets are not the same as racial ones or those that scorn particular erotic predilections, if only because sexual epithets cleave, and cleave to, the private and public realms profoundly. Queer and nigger, in their unreconstructed, homophobic and racist contexts, have no private dimension, except in terms of the hateful chatter among themselves of homophobes and racists. However, a woman, in intimate circumstances with a woman or a man, may invoke her pussy, or may thrill at hearing it invoked. All dirty talk is uniquely sweet in this context, and pussy is the sweetest dirty word in the English lexicon of heterosexual and lesbian intimacy.

In the halls of the maternity ward, women strolled gingerly in their motley robes. Most were young, in their mid-twenties; none wore make-up. Their hair was a little wild. All were pale, and shuffled as though each step required consideration. They were sore, but needed to move a bit, to "walk it off," as grizzled coaches recommend after solid hits.

Some pushed shopping carts lined with linen and wool, their tiny ones swaddled within. Some paused to sit on benches lining the halls while family and young men fawned over the carts. All seemed to realize that they'd accomplished something marvelous; they smiled wearily, or stared off. Everyone was hushed.

The Czech word for pussy is *piča* (PEEcha). It doesn't have the association with a cute animal, but is similarly capable of conveying the sense of diminutive endearment. Each woman gingerly pacing the halls of that *Porodnice*, on *Apolinářská ulice* in Praha 2, realized that everyone around her—other women similarly tender and ensconced within the ugly but comforting walls of the sprawled building; the new *babičkas*, grandmothers who will be much more involved in their grandchildren's upbringing than the grandmothers of their far-flung American cousins usually are in theirs; the new, as well as seasoned, fathers humbled by the sheer single-minded purpose of the place; and personnel: scant doctors, ubiquitous nurses and cooks and cleaners—all of them, felt something that should only be called reverence for her *piča*, that object of desire that transforms by such violence into cosmic threshold. (It is said that "*Praha*," Prague, in the ancient Slavonic tongue may have meant "threshold.")

The Czech language, my teenage daughter tells me, is more intimate than English. I trust her judgments regarding the differences between the two languages and cultures more than those of anyone else I know, even those of her mother, whose PhD in comparative linguistics and literature makes her no slouch in such matters. But my daughter has grown up speaking both languages, being educated on both sides of the Atlantic, and so is a bifurcated being, and she says Czech is an intimate language, that that's how she hears, lives, and feels it. She said once what I have always suspected from my own scant comprehension, that Czech doesn't resonate as public discourse the way English does. The example she gives is how silly the talking heads reading the news on TV sometimes sound to her, broadcasting information in official tones that seem artificial compared with what issues from American and British talking heads. It seems that English allows dramatic contrast between public and private speech, accommodates an intrinsic difference between them, to an extent that Czech cannot, at least to the ear of a Czech-American girl in her mid teens.

However, even I can hear the diminutives, and diminutives within diminutives, that constitute so much of Czech talk. One needn't give a friend a little gift, a *malý dárek*, but rather a *dáreček*, and almost anything can similarly be made small and dear, a car *(autíčko)*, a house in the country *(chatička)*, food *(mlíčko)*, even a politician *(Havlíček)* or a housefly *(muška)*. Every name can be made diminutive and thereby intimate, sweet, endearing. This is not to say that Czechs are adorable; they certainly don't perceive themselves as particularly so. They are, in fact, in public quite dour, sometimes even forbidding. But when they are among family and friends there is always the potential, linguistically, for endearments that enfold the very names of things, requiring no adjectival assistance.

In the *Velký česko-anglický slovník*, "*piča*" ("*pička*," diminutive) is "*(f, vulg: am.)* pussy, twat." Felines and flora are not even mentioned. In the *Merriam-Webster*, that most American of dictionaries, pussy is an adjective for cat and willow; its primary designation, in the hearts and minds of Americans of every ethnicity and social class, is a ringing silence.

I cannot walk the streets of Prague with my daughters and not wonder how they are processing the images of females on billboards. Here, sexual associations with commercial products are even more blatant, even more frankly puerile than in America. Images of women all but naked are linked to just about everything, from cars to garden tools. And yet the social context for such linkages is as different as Puritanism from Communism.

The Puritans were the source of sexual repression in the service of the vaunted work ethic; the Party was the source of sexual repression in the service of the ideal of gender equality within the collective. The Puritans were wildly successful at fucking up sexuality; the Commies were miserable failures. Regarding the former, lust was evil; regarding the latter, lust was bourgeois, which is to say evil stripped of supernatural authority. The cultures they engendered, emerging in different epochs and under radically different circumstances, determined present attitudes toward desire and its commercial uses. And these attitudes are haunted to different effect by the ideologies that engendered them.

In the case of American culture, a middle-aged breast exposed on primetime becomes an icon of Puritanical prohibition even as the industry churns out, unchecked and unabated, rap and hip-hop (some of it, and much of pop music in general), at its worst, the most misogynous and puerile cultural product ever conceived. In the case of Czech culture, a tried and true marketing strategy runs rampant against a recent past in which markets as such were *verboten*. I would argue that the effect of Puritanism on American commercial culture is more pernicious, in terms of the female body's iconic role, than the effect of Communism on Czech commercial culture. For one thing, the former is longer-lived and more obfuscated and contradictory.

And this obfuscating contradiction is accomplished by canny compartmentalization, precisely the trick of all psychic repression. A bare breast on primetime is bad; misogynous rap is bad but contained within its own commercial ghetto. "Fuck" and other nasty words are forbidden on network, contained on cable. In cinema, degrees of titillation are contained within a rating system, and the pornography industry itself is as specialized, which is to say compartmentalized, as any component of the military-industrial complex. In America, the only aspect of life that is not contained, cordoned off, is precisely that which should be, the private life. And so, paradoxically, we are ultimately contained: we live in glass houses, psychically naked. When we dance, we do so in a music video. We live on TV, in both senses of sustenance and containment.

When my girls see the female body at once idealized and objectified to commercial ends in America they are seeing something different from what they see in Central Europe when it is similarly displayed. In America, it is something lurid doing the dirty but necessary work of selling. In Central Europe they are seeing an ironic parody of that, and they seem to *get* the irony, which has to do simply with the fact that the erotic has not been linked with evil in the Czech psyche, at least for most of the twentieth century; the private realm, for Czechs, since the end of the First Republic, has been the location of freedom, and all flagrantly sexual activities have been political, albeit ironic, acts of opposition.

The location of freedom in the West, especially in America, is the public realm, the marketplace in which everything, *everything* is for sale in its proper stall, its compartment, in the vast bazaar. And the private realm is house arrest, at least in the sense that our private behaviors are determined by the requirements of the marketplace. We buy our public freedom with our private lives; this equation is possible only in the context of Puritan prohibitions that are instruments not of denial but of guilt, the solvent in which our manufactured desires are suspended. It's guilt that

renders so much nasty, lurid, *falsely* prohibited. It's guilt that pro-
duces the psychic resistance, like a dam to a torrent of desire,
creating the power of the great market economy.

One of the cable stations in Prague is called *Private Gold*. It's
hardcore porn and is scrambled for non-subscribers. I pass it
flipping between the Czech stations that are clumped at the
beginning of the queue, and English-language news stations—
CNN, CNBC, BBC—at the end. It comes on late, after the girls
are in bed. Sometimes I pause because, well, who wouldn't? I've
never been particularly interested in porn, in fact have always
marveled that guys could be so, shall we say, dependent upon it.
Sometimes, on the scrambled porn station, for, literally, a fraction
of a second, a glorious close-up of a shaved, wholly exposed vagina
will flash. Then the scramble will re-engage and if I keep it there
for a few more seconds, I can witness, within the frantic scramble,
a steady bobbing that can only be a head working back and forth
or a buttock likewise.

I find it hilarious, though not un-erotic. The scramble is, in
some ways, more erotic than if the images were unabashed, and,
of course, this fact is the secret of the erotic. Porn isn't erotic; it's
anti-erotic, merely instrumental. On the other hand, arousal is an
incidental feature of erotica, which is much more about mystery,
about the mystery of the other, that which is delightfully unknow-
able. Peering into the scramble of *Private Gold*, I am usually not
aroused, though sometimes mildly so, titillated, but I am always,
after the ten-second pause before transport to the world's woes on
cable news, to a special report on sex trafficking in Europe or
punishment of women under the Taliban, a little sad.

It's a father's sadness, for I know that this is the world I must
prepare my girls for, one in which male lust is fed images,

scrambled and not, of women submitting to everything, and one in which women are swathed from head to feet to protect males from the sight of them. It is a world in which children are sold to men for sex, and families murder sisters and daughters for being raped. It is a world in which female children are "circumcised," and solicited for sex on the Internet.

At the public pool near Vyšehrad, on the main road along the Vltava, the grassy field between the rusty hill there and the two Olympic-size pools is covered, summer days, with hundreds of bodies, and most of the women, young and old, are topless, as is the case on all the European beaches we've visited. My daughters notice that in American bathing areas women are never topless, and they notice generally that the human body is differently regarded in Europe and America. I'll leave it to them to articulate that difference for themselves, and for the world, as they determine over the course of their lives what part of them is Czech, what European, and what American.

And as they name their parts in that respect, may they establish the appropriate distances between their bodies and the world; may they assume comfortable relations, within their languages, with their bodies, relations unmediated by the sexist iconography of the marketplace, which is to say by mere titillation.

The two nurses who attended the birth were young and had sweet faces. In Czech, a nurse is a *sestra,* sister, and there was a familial tenderness to their ministrations. They worked around me; my job was simply to allow Dominika to dig her nails into the flesh of my hand and forearm, bruising and drawing a little blood. They clearly enjoyed their work, casting knowing smiles at one another as the contractions, measured below the baby's heart-beat on a monitor, became more frequent. One wobbled the belly

to keep the baby awake; the other reminded Dom to breathe stac-
cato by doing so herself. At what must have been the exactly
appropriate moment, they helped Dom off the bed onto a large
rubber ball and told her to bounce a little. Doing so seemed to
relieve the pain, but also hastened the delivery, because when it
began it was furious.

When I was a boy, pussy was Heaven. When I was a young
man, it was sweet and earthly succor. At the moment when the
Czech sister twisted the body of my Czech-American daughter
from the dilated womb, and presented her to my view, as a waiter
presents a wine, and I witnessed the baby's sex, I thought, ridiculously, of those wooden dolls within dolls within dolls within
dolls within dolls that Russian entrepreneurs hawked on Prague's
side streets right after the Velvet Revolution, along with caviar
and Soviet military paraphernalia. I thought of the final tiny
figure that is somehow the point.

A Brief History of Fine Dining

RECENTLY, MY DAUGHTERS AND I DINED at a favorite restaurant in Prague 4. It's on our walking route, uphill, to Vyšehrad Park, where we take Ellie, the two-year-old, to romp in a play space among the trees. Sometimes, before or after romping, the girls and I will have lunch or dinner in that restaurant, which is attached to a football pitch, a very odd and interesting arrangement. Every other time we'd dined at the soccer place, as I think of it, the food had been good and the service adequate. The last time we dined there, however, was horrendous. The service was criminally bad, and I, and the girls, had a sneaking suspicion that our speaking English among ourselves was the reason. In the twilight of George Bush's reign, it is sometimes not easy being an American abroad. My girls rattled on to the waiter, when he finally deigned to approach the table, but I spoke to him in English because I feel foolish creaking out my scant Czech when accompanied by my native-speaking children who wince at my terrible accent, and, besides, I was feeling defiant. I wanted to leave, but the girls were famished.

Because I waited tables at haughty, four-star restaurants in the French Quarter of New Orleans through the late seventies and early eighties; because I wore a tuxedo and was slim and good-looking; because I took my job somewhat seriously, was pretty good at it, and made decent money, I am less tolerant than most of shoddy service, and more tolerant of situations in which a server is a victim of circumstances beyond her or his control. Our waiter that afternoon was a dumpy, dour, balding mid-life *Švejk* of a man, probably a decade younger than I but already feeling old and left behind. He had five tables working and was handling the others just fine; indeed, two of the parties had entered after us and were already being served their drinks and appetizers. Ellie, the best two-year-old on the planet, was bouncing from lap to lap, Ema's to Annie's and back to mine, and venturing to a corner by the table to scratch something gooey, with a spoon, that was caked there. I eyed her to make sure she didn't eat what she was scraping, but otherwise was simply thankful that hunger was not making her cranky.

I gave our waiter numerous Evil Eyes, but his head did not explode and he did not drop to the floor holding his crotch and screaming. When he finally took our drink orders we, of course, also gave him our food orders, not wanting to chance another delay. Twenty minutes later he delivered our drinks, and the wrong soups, which, of course, we ate. During the ice age before our entrées arrived, I told stories about my days as a waiter.

Annie wanted to know what "fine dining" means, and if that place was it. I told her no, on a good day it was a nice little restaurant, but it wasn't fine dining. Does it mean the food is better? Well, not necessarily, but usually. Is it just fancier? Yeah, that's it; it's fancier. Then we recalled some of the fine restaurants in which we'd dined, and were surprised to realize that one of the few fine dining experiences we'd had in Prague, and indeed the most recent one, was at the nearby Holiday Inn, a chain that in the

US is more strongly associated with extra-marital rendezvous than haute cuisine.

I was beginning to admire our waiter. Executing such shoddy treatment actually requires effort. First of all, it requires conspiracy with the kitchen. I imagined him telling the cook that a long-haired, muscled-up American asshole and his Czech-speaking brats were on B-3. *Let's slow roll the so'bitch. Let's mess up his afternoon for the sake of all innocent Iraqi people, for the sake of all of Europe and Asia, for the whole damned world. Maybe, soon, the baby will begin to cry from hunger. Maybe he'll pay for their drinks and leave. Surely they will leave.*

But the girls and I were settled in. They, especially Annie, are as stubborn as I, almost as stubborn as their mother, my ex-wife, who becomes a half-buried boulder when she is of a mind to win. And Ellie was munching bread from a basket we'd pirated from another table, excavating meticulously the tiny tar pit she'd discovered nearly an hour earlier.

I suddenly wished to be nowhere else on earth than on that glassed-in restaurant patio, with my glorious daughters, waiting for sustenance that may never arrive, or may arrive having been spat on by the cook and his helpers and the waiter and maybe the bartender, too. Perhaps my *Losos Provencal*, served in aluminum foil and dripping herbs, would be horribly fouled, but I doubted it. The waiter, I could tell because I am gifted at making such judgments, was not evil, was not even mean, really. He had simply dismissed us, as waiters sometimes will. He was in a position of power, and, after initially screwing up quite by accident, realized I wasn't going to give him one of those ridiculously large American tips, anyway, so he simply didn't give a damn how long we sat. Of course, I strode twice from the sun-bright patio into the smoke-rich gloomy interior, where I stood in the middle of the room and shrugged hugely, palms up, my face screwed into a mask of incredulity. My server stared through me, smoking a cigarette, leaning on the bar, waiting, I assumed, for someone else's order.

But the girls were fine. We'd finished eons ago those soups we'd not ordered, but we had plenty of bread, having swiped a second basket, and Ellie was surely on the verge of revealing something truly marvelous under that crud. Ema pressed me further regarding fine dining, how one distinguishes it from that which is not "fine" but very good, and, if, as I'd earlier suggested, a very bad restaurant can be said to offer a "fine" dining experience and an excellent restaurant not, how "fancy" does a restaurant have to be to deserve the designation of "fine."

I suggested that the designation of "fine" may be clouding the broader, more salient issue as to what "dining" and "dining out" mean, though surely "fine dining" is the ideal. I told her it has to do with fear of death, and with formality, the innate belief that by creating order, especially around so primal an activity as eating, chaos and death may be cheated.

In the beginning there was hunger. The whole world was a buffet. One bellied up, or died trying. Hunting and gathering, an acquired taste for carrion, the first canny weapons, and, of course, fire and its divine cousins—the magic permeating all stuff—conspired to define gender roles exquisitely toward "Here-and-There," Here being where females kept camp and There being where males had to go to get meat, one way or another. "Here" is where the first restaurant work began.

Restaurants are cathedrals of domesticity, of here-ness, of comfort. They are matriarchal spaces. With agriculture came patriarchy, and the earth, all fecund dirt, turned into a woman, and women got the famous raw deal. And of course they've still got it, though in some quarters it's being renegotiated.

Restaurant work parallels prostitution, both of which dovetail with the institution of slavery, the key to human "progress." For, when one population (or gender) could compel another to live in its midst and tend to its most basic needs and desires, the sky became the limit to human brutality and ingenuity. So that's where the single god got stuck, in the sky, and "we" all became "His" restaurant; we *served* Him. Jesus Christ was divine gratuity.

Though one may suppose, too, that "fine dining" has roots in Leviticus, in all dietary laws, in animal sacrifice, in ritual killing and contagion magic. That is, it has the same roots as lyric poetry, and both are just two of the more important things we do, after sex ("after" in both senses), about our terror of extinction.

If something is "fine" it is free of impurities, though in the phrase it is closer to "fine arts," which are concerned with the creation of beautiful objects and performances. In the case of fine dining, the goal is a beautiful condition, a fleeting beauty. Yet the connection to metallurgy shouldn't be ruled out; that is, the sense in which "beauty" as a condition immanent in an object, as well as suffusing a particular kind of situation both link to the practical circumstance of impurities being removed from a metal. At the core of (daddy-centered) civilization, the essence of beauty is linked to purity, and the traditional notion of beauty has always had this fascist bent. It is therefore a huge historical paradox that one of the great accomplishments of High Modernism, for example, was to un-tether purity from beauty, though it often did so in the name of fascist agendas.

Well, pound for (Ezra) Pound, beauty and purity are never far apart. It is at least interesting to note that, before the 1989 revolutions that laughed Communism toward the great (and now ironic) ashbin of history Trotsky made famous, there were no "fine" restaurants behind the Iron Curtain, certainly not in Prague, exclusive Party establishments notwithstanding. Fine dining requires class difference; it thrives on the complexity of human relations along class lines, and is particularly dependent upon the existence of a broad and thriving bourgeoisie—that is, a lot of people with money, but not enough to afford servants.

Fine dining isn't a single lie, but a little nest of several. The first lie is of discernment—which means it centers on whether most bourgeois patrons are capable of making judgments based on fine distinctions of taste. No more than perhaps one in ten folks who can afford to dine at fine establishments on a regular basis can distinguish between excellence and mediocrity. This is the primary reason Western Civilization is likely doomed, but that's another matter. Most good and great restaurants cast pearls before duplicitous swine who are only fooling themselves. Every real chef knows this, and most waiters learn to play upon this fact.

The second lie of fine dining is civility. All children learn quickly that "good manners" are lies of convenience; as adults we learn that civility is a lie of necessity. In fine dining, civility, that pillar of the Status Quo, is what gives cohesion to the formalities, the artifice, of the dining experience. In every social negotiation, every non-violent conflict, codes of civility determine behavior. In fine dining, the dance between those serving and those being served apes the one between Old World aristocracy and its servants, Old South gentry and its slaves. And yet in almost every instance a good chef will feel superior to her or his patrons, as will the waiters, and as will especially the maître d'. The essence of the civility of fine dining is the lie of the power relation: a good or excellent restaurant will always feel superior to its constituency. A truly fine restaurant doesn't serve the ninety percent of its patrons who can't discern excellence from mediocrity; it merely humors them.

The third lie of fine dining is customer infallibility, for the restaurant customer, unlike in most other commercial relations, is almost always wrong. The fourth lie is hygiene. All restaurants—all—are filthy places. That's the primary reason the lights are kept low. They're petri dishes. One may wonder why more people don't die from eating out. It's possible that more do than we imagine, especially in New Orleans.

How many times did I witness a cook on the line scratch himself with buttery fingers, leaving a greasy swatch on his neck or cheek, then continue rolling the redfish fillet in cayenne? How many cockroaches did I observe fall from smoke vents into deep fryers? How many dead rodents did I step on as I scrounged through pantries for supplies? How many live ones? How many chefs did I glimpse picking their noses unabashedly in the midst of a night's work? Does anyone really think waiters always wash their hands when they return to dining rooms from toilets? Most don't out of healthy contempt for the undiscerning ninety percent, none of whom should want to know how much their food gets handled, literally, in the kitchen. Any truly professional waiter is profoundly aware that there's nothing "pure" about fine dining; everything's contaminated, at least a little.

Discernment. Civility. Customer infallibility. Hygiene. The little nest of lies that is fine dining, the history of which is the history of beauty.

Someone other than our waiter brought our food, a cheerless mouse of a woman who'd worked the other end of the patio, but now everyone but my girls and I had left. The sun was going down beyond the pitch, and Ellie postponed her dig. The girls devoured, speaking little. Ema, a vegetarian, commented that her pasta and steamed broccoli with a light dill sauce was excellent. I cut Annie's steak into tiny pieces, and she ate around the knife and fork as I worked. The salmon was the best I'd had in America or Europe; it was perfect. Ellie, our genius angel baby, was camped on my lap eating my perfect salmon with me, and a side of golden croquettes.

School in Nature

REGARDING MY DAUGHTERS, I WORRY THAT I'm over-protective
almost as often as I worry that I am not protective enough. These
worries register differently in America and in Europe. In the United
States, in New Orleans or Kalamazoo, I worry daily, hourly, for my
daughters' physical safety. In America, men creep through windows
to brutalize, then drag away and murder, little girls. In America,
girls and boys should not be on the streets unattended, should not
play beyond the gaze of caring adults. In Prague, women, even
teenage girls, may traverse the streets after dark. My teenager scoots
about the city on public transport, the terrific metro and tram systems, without fear. There are monsters everywhere; children are
stolen, hurt, and killed everywhere, even in Prague, though much,
much less frequently than in American cities and environs.

Both of my girls have commented as to how different it feels
to live on the two continents, different in terms of safety, feeling
safe. The ten-year-old insists that I am "over-protective" generally,
but particularly so in America. My sixteen-year-old says that
she herself doesn't feel safe in the United States, though she
understands that she may be responding as much to my and her
mother's sense of threat as manifesting her own.

I recall standing a couple of years ago with my daughters' Czech mother, before we divorced, waving at Annie as she and a busload of her eight-year-old compatriots began their journey eighty kilometers outside of Prague to *"škola v přírodě,"* "School in Nature." She would spend a week there, sleeping in a dormitory, taking three hardy squares daily, studying a little but playing a lot "in nature," which is simply to say nowhere near a paved street and in the midst of much organic stuff. There would be hiking and organized play. Perhaps they would learn about which mushrooms, *houby*, are edible and which will make you nauseous. I recall hoping she would learn to tell time with a stick, though she was not yet very swift to read time on a clock face. We could only dream that she would be infused with good domestic habits "in nature" that she all but laughs at us for trying to instill in her at home.

As the bus pulled from the curb, over twenty sets of parents—and, remarkably, both a mother and father accompanied almost every child—waved goodbye; one had tears in her eyes. She was a red-cheeked dumpling of a woman whose head was completely bald, no doubt less a fashion statement than the result of chemo. All of the parents twitched a little or fussed with toddlers, suppressing, it seemed, tiny trepidations. No one expected anything bad to happen to any of the children on that bus; indeed, "School in Nature" is a regular feature of public elementary schooling in the Czech Republic, beginning in daycare. Every late spring, kids are packed off to the country for a week to bond with their classmates and teachers in a more expansive and intimate setting than the classroom.

Do children four to eight years old get bundled off, say, to summer camps in America? When they do, aren't parents usually heavily involved? I mean, imagine even a single school district, much less an entire state, or the entire nation, procuring the infrastructure to accommodate such an event, and then imagine fifty or so families (in this case, two second grade classes) on a given day sending off such young children to a place they've never seen and will likely never see, to be cared for by individuals who, with the exception of the classroom teacher, they have never met and will likely never meet. Do American parents of very young children harbor that much trust? In America I wouldn't; here I do, but mainly because everyone else does.

Around that time, I attended a lecture at the American Embassy's Woodrow Wilson Center. A fellow from a middling Southern university, on some sort of Fulbright tour of US embassies, gave a talk on the contemporary American novel. I immediately disliked him for numerous reasons: his sensible suit; his pissy, condescending demeanor; the fact that he thought German was Kafka's second language; his bald assertion that Pynchon is the greatest living American writer; and the first page of his handout, a list of MacArthur "Genius Grant" winners, with Pynchon's and three or four other names in bold type; but I disliked him primarily because he listed off the top of his head several "popular" novels, among them *The Lovely Bones* by Alice Sebold, about which he said, with an actual sigh, "It really isn't very good, is it?"

No, it isn't: for one, the second half is contrived, oddly predictable. But the first half is brilliant; Sebold found a way to make the subject of extreme brutality against female children palatable to an American, predominately female, audience. By entering the realm of the fantastic, by soldering Mickey Mouse ears onto Ted Bundy, by bringing the most infantile and banal elements of American popular culture to bear upon the most hideous features of that culture, Sebold made it possible for Americans, but especially American women, to consume, in all its hideous details, the brutal murder of a child.

The narrator is the murdered adolescent Susie Salmon, as even most folks who haven't read the novel probably know by now. There's much prattle throughout about a goofy heaven she now occupies, the rules of engagement between the dead and the living. But Sebold does not spare the reader the details of the crime, the protracted suffering of the victim, and the reader, the target audience for the novel, is female. Is it the first novel by a woman, aimed at a female audience, which is about the most extreme violence against female children? If it isn't, there can't be many others that depend upon the reader feeling empathy for the child victim at the moment of victimization, depend upon the reader projecting herself into the victim's consciousness at the moment a hideously violent crime is being committed. Indeed, how many novels by American women have centered on explicit, fatal violence against female children? I can't think of a single work of fiction, whose primary audience is female, which centers on the detailed revelation of such violence. The fact that it could only be done in the realm of the fantastic; that it could only reach its audience by asserting that death is not death; that it could only stare unflinchingly into the maw of a child's doom by giving that child a most implausible life after death, stabs me in the heart, my father heart. *The Lovely Bones* is a mediocre novel that touches greatness by accomplishing something Pynchon's writing never has and never will; it gives an authentic voice to those who have been silenced, authentic not in a literary sense because the point of view of the novel is sophomoric; authentic rather, in the sense that it speaks passionately to the deepest need for wish fulfillment, the wish that the world, that American society, be other than it is, regarding children, especially.

There is art that flies below the intellect's radar; this is true of much popular art, MTV stuff, Hollywood stuff. But a novel like *The Lovely Bones* is not "popular"; it occupies an interesting zone, though, one that is broader than the elite audience for such authors as Pynchon, Barth, and DeLillo certainly, but not, I would argue, any less sophisticated, just less professional in its tastes, less self-conscious and condescending, certainly less hierarchical. There are novels, such as *Gravity's Rainbow*, that are great in spite of being fodder for jaded academic discourse, and mediocre novels that manage to ride the slipstream of a national dream or nightmare. It is the latter that somehow get under the skin, and burrow deep into the dreambox of the psyche, as do myths and fairytales.

A father's fear for his daughters can be debilitating, for him as well as for the female children. In nature, gender roles are fixed; in human society, because it is human nature to stand at once in and out of nature, roles result from generations of tough negotiations. A reflective person cannot be an American father of females and not be, in the most fundamental sense, feminist, even if he considers himself a social conservative, which I do not. There cannot be many among those who consider themselves social conservatives who do not wish their daughters to have opportunities equal to their sons' to pursue career goals, to earn the educations that will enable them to have desired careers and social status. And certainly those same fathers want society to be organized such that daughters do not have to run life-long gauntlets of physical threat. But since all women, in America especially, must indeed run such a gauntlet, what is a father's role in preparing his daughter for life-long physical threat? The powerful desire to protect runs counter to a father's feminist ideals. To protect a female, or, more precisely to be "overly protective," as my ten-year-old has learned to say, is to fall back into the patriarchal paradigm, but to speak practically, and not just ideologically, how can a female child learn to negotiate the gauntlet, to survive it, to thrive in spite of it, when she is being protected, even "overly protected," by her father?

No daughter of mine would ever be allowed to walk the route from school that the narrator of *The Lovely Bones* is allowed to traverse daily; it is a route similar to ones that millions of adolescent girls routinely take to and from school, to and from friends' houses, and the parents of those girls are not bad parents, of course; they're playing the odds, as everyone every day must play odds, tempt fate, at least a little. But I am constitutionally unable to play those particular odds regarding my daughters. I will not allow my teenager to walk by herself anywhere that is not heavily peopled. At what point will I loosen up? At what point will I, too, play the odds?

When she herself insists. She has, until now, never complained about a lack of mobility, a lack of physical freedom in America. But I do worry that I have conditioned her to require my protection, to prefer protection to freedom, and how, thus conditioned, will she learn to run the gauntlet? Will she simply require another male to "protect" her after she has left home?

My daughters, especially my teenager, love nature shows; they watch the National Geographic channel on Czech cable, and are unfazed by mating beasts; they also thrill to see the lioness drag down the gazelle from behind. They root for the lioness, love that it is she who hunts for the pride while the old guy, in all his grouchy, maned glory, sits on his haunches blinking out over the killing field. They are not sentimental about the prey, and that is good, I think. When a couple of years ago I threatened to drop the girls' guinea pigs off on a grassy plot in Vyšehrad Park, near our home in Prague 4, my then eight-year-old, of course, knew that the animals would probably be immediately devoured by cats, but called my bluff; I said, "Annie, you know they'll be eaten, right?" to which she replied, "That's only natural." I continued to clean her pets' cage, grumbling about how little she attends to them.

The problem arises when we tolerate violence against females as somehow natural, simply a nasty aspect of the order of things. And that is precisely what has happened in America. We tolerate what seems natural, what simply seems nature's dark side. European society generally, and certainly Czech society specifically, in ideological terms are more sexist than American society; the feminist hue and cry has been loudest and most effective as ideology, which is to say as rhetoric, as social discourse, in America. But in the developed world, in the vaunted West, America is also the most dangerous environment for females. It is quite simply the case that my daughters are more physically free in Europe, and more rhetorically free in America.

I lived for ten years with a woman who had been brutally raped a year before we came together. It was the late seventies, and she and a workmate were traveling from New Orleans to somewhere near Hattiesburg, Mississippi, as I recall, to visit colleagues on a holiday. Their car broke down somewhere on the highway to Hattiesburg; three men in a pickup stopped. She and her friend climbed into the flatbed, but instead of driving them to the next gas station, the truck turned off the highway into the woods.

What they did to her, what it took her years to describe to me in full, lying in the dark, weeping, often intoxicated, was beyond description, literally. That is, it is the sort of event, the sort of experience, a systematic, even ritualistic humiliation and terrorizing that must never be appropriated, in any manner. I mention it here obliquely simply to celebrate her heroism, her maintenance of dignity, her humbling grace, and to speak briefly to the effect such an act may have upon a man who loves a woman who has been thus victimized.

She never sought counseling, never received the disinterested care anyone who has experienced such brutality should. In the midst of the attack, she'd been certain that when they were through with her they'd kill her, and, thereafter, on occasion, expressed the sentiment that she wished they had indeed swiftly killed her there, among the trees.

She got better. She healed, in a fashion. We loved each other, in a fashion. We were young, living in the French Quarter, working in restaurants between stints in graduate school until I finally found a teaching job in New Orleans. Perhaps I was even more tender toward her than I otherwise would have been, more attendant. She was the most poised and beautiful person I'd ever known, and I wanted to kill the evil bastards who'd hurt her. I fantasized coming upon them, individually, and beating each one to death with my fists, choking life out of them. Such revenge was utterly impossible, of course. She hadn't officially reported the attack. The evil was untraceable.

She certainly didn't thereafter make a secret of the rape, so my referencing it here breaks no confidence. It didn't define our relationship; it didn't siphon all joy from her life, our lives. There was much laughter, much fun. But no day passed without my thinking about it, without my feeling that surge of anger, the desire to destroy physically the men who had brutalized someone so beautiful.

Which is to say I wanted to destroy myself, that part of me that was culpable, that part of every man that is culpable. I would bring brutality to bear upon brutality, and thereby sanctify it.

The gauntlet my daughters must learn to negotiate is organized according to the same imperatives by which I would protect them. I would traverse the border from Nature to Nurture even as my girls must learn to straddle it. And that haughty, ignorant professor of wholly irrelevant, hierarchical judgments, even as I judge him so coldly, perhaps unfairly, should renegotiate his relation to whatever canon he prays to, so that he knows a truly original book by a woman, for other women, when he stumbles over it.

Katie's Hair

SEVERAL YEARS AGO, BEFORE BARACK OBAMA saved the world from an affable idiot and his evil handlers, Annie had a crush on a cute kid named Chris Brown, the heartthrob *du jour* of girls nine to nineteen. She was nine going on nineteen, a Disney Channel aficionado, and, though I tried to limit her exposure to that world in which fathers are stooges and teenage girls set the agenda regarding just about everything, she consumed enough of it to have absorbed its ethos. The six months each year she lived in Prague, Disney Channel was the only thing, other than friends, for which she expressed any yearning. Chris Brown she could access on MTV in Prague (she now calls him a pig for beating Rhianna), but Hilary Duff and Raven were an ocean away. I remember it seemed a little odd that they weren't dubbed and run on Czech stations (to her great credit, Annie hates it when favorite movies and sitcoms get dubbed), given that so much of the worst American television is indeed dubbed and aired on the Czech Republic's four stations. Besides MTV, the other English-language cable channels available in Prague are Discovery, CNN, CNBC, Eurosport, and BBC News, in other words, stuff I will deign to flick glances at a couple hours a day with my laptop on my knees, but which holds no interest for her.

One interesting feature of both Disney Channel and MTV, of which I heartily approve, is the representation of minorities. Annie has grown up on both sides of the Atlantic with the powerful multicultural influence of MTV, which in so many other ways, not the least of which are puerile wantonness and occasional misogyny, is pernicious; Disney Channel, once her exclusively American pleasure, is simply banal. Yet both are fiercely, and gloriously, multicultural. Annie has grown up assuming that, despite the unvarnished racism of Czech society and a vague sense of America's Original Sin of slavery, the world is a place where people of different skin tones and ethnicities can and should have fun together.

So it was not at all surprising, after Annie announced her best friend to be Katie, that I would not learn Katie is African-American until I actually met her while picking Annie up from school one day. I'd heard about Katie for a couple of weeks, knew that she loved Chris Brown, that she watched the same Disney Channel shows as Annie, that she had two brothers, that her father didn't live with the family, and that she was considerably smaller than Annie, but not that she was "dark" (wholly unprompted, Annie says "dark" rather than "black" or "brown," and, for example, says that I, her Irish-Greek father am a "little dark," certainly compared to her own blond, blue-eyed self). Katie's mother and I, over the months, negotiated several play dates and one sleepover to be conducted at my condo in downtown Kalamazoo. Katie was a terrific kid, polite but frank, and usually didn't let Annie dominate her as Annie tends to dominate, often quite sweetly though sometimes not, everyone else in her sphere.

On one weekend play day Annie announced that she was going to wash and play with Katie's hair. Of course, alarm bells sounded, and I suggested that Katie's mother probably has a pretty strict routine regarding Katie's very pretty, obviously tended-to hair, and that the girls should probably play with something other than each other's 'dos.

Katie nonchalantly said that her mother wouldn't care if Annie washed and played with her hair, and I said that I should still wait to hear Katie's mother say that it would be okay for Annie to wash and mess with it. Well, they wore me down, and, against my better judgment, I relented.

It was stupid and irresponsible of me to relent. A nine-year-old visiting her strong-willed friend in her friend's own home will naturally want to please the other girl and will not exercise sound judgment in such matters.

I recalled my best friend in sixth grade, Jesse, who lived three blocks from the government housing projects where my mother, four siblings, and I resided during my father's second incarceration. Jesse was one of seven children, and his family lived in a big house they owned. His father had a truck, and embarked on long hauls every fortnight or so, returning a few days before the next haul. He must have made decent money because his family lived well. Jesse's mother was a large, loud, funny woman who liked me, and probably pitied me because she often asked me to eat with her family, and later invited me to spend the night, which I loved to do. Life was not good at home. My mother had been diagnosed to have multiple sclerosis, suffered seizures, and could barely walk; there was often not enough to eat in the house, and the man who had been my mother's lover had left us in the knowledge that my father would be getting out of prison soon. I don't recall how much of this Jesse's mother was privy to, but she could certainly see from how I dressed, probably from the look in my eyes, and how skinny I was, that life at home was not good. She certainly knew that I lived in the projects.

After a hearty breakfast of pancakes and sausage or eggs and bacon, as much as I and everyone else in the house could eat, I'd sit and talk to Jesse's mother while she lined her four daughters up to do their hair. It would take more than an hour, was an intricate task, and she was deft at it, could look at me and around the room while she manipulated a girl's hair and talked and laughed, working a substance into it I can't recall except for the sweet smell, a little like jasmine. She held bobby pins in the corners of her mouth.

Annie washed Katie's hair in my bathroom sink, making remarkably little mess. Then she sat Katie on a stool in front of the TV, and worked her hair with a brush and comb as the two of them watched an episode (one they'd obviously seen before) of *The Suite Life of Zack & Cody,* a Disney Channel staple about twin boys who live in a hotel with their lounge-singer mother.

When Annie finished (I worked in my room for the hour they took over the living room), I was horrified. Katie's hair was shaped rather like the big bumps on that Mouseketeer hat Annette Funicello wore so fetchingly. Given that, according to my arrangement with her mother, we only had fifteen or twenty minutes to return Katie by car to her home, I had no time for damage control, and I could tell from Katie's eyes as she peered into the mirror over the couch that bleak consequences awaited her.

Driving to her home, I flicked glances at the girls in the rearview mirror. Both were somber; Annie correctly interpreted Katie's quiet, and the fact that she wrapped her sweater around her head, to mean that the coiffure Annie had sculpted with comb and brush and gel (the latter I hadn't noticed, alas) was, perhaps, ahead of its time.

Consistent with all the other drop-offs but this time with a little cowardice feathered in, I stayed in the car as Annie walked Katie to the door. The smaller girl disappeared into the living room light.

We hadn't driven a quarter mile before my cell phone rang. Katie's mother was beside herself, calm but clearly livid. I apologized from the soles of my feet, and confessed that I'd been stupid to take a nine-year-old's word on such a matter and under such circumstances. She asked me if Katie played with Annie's hair, or did Annie treat Katie "like a little Barbie doll."

It was a remarkable moment. I understood precisely what she meant, and could imagine little white girls fifty, a hundred years ago in the South "playing" with the children of maids or nannies, how the power relation in such play must have mirrored that of adult relations, how a little white girl might indeed treat her black playmate not as an equal in play, not as a subject, but as an object, a doll, even.

I assured her that on other occasions I'd watched Katie fussing with Annie's hair, and Annie chimed affirmation from the backseat. But I also told her that I knew her point was well taken, that I understood her concern, though I'm not sure she understood that I actually could understand.

In my relationship to Jesse's family, class trumped race; I was poor white. They were relatively affluent black. Had I lived in the nice house and Jesse in the projects, would our friendship have worked? Would my mother have invited Jesse into our home?

My mother would have, though I don't know if I'd have had the social skills to form a bond with a black kid from the projects, one on welfare and whose father was in prison. Even in 1965, kids on welfare in the projects, whose fathers were incarcerated, were much more likely to be black than white.

I'd probably not have had the social skills, or the occasion, to form such a friendship. I can't recall how my friendship with Jesse began. I'm just now recalling his last name, Johnson, and that his mother had named her seventh child, still in a crib during that period when the family took me in, Lyndon Baines, and informed the White House by letter that she'd named her baby after the president; she received a letter back thanking her, and she showed it to me. But I don't recall the names of any of the other siblings, though I do remember that Jesse's youngest sister, two or three years old, really liked me, would sit on my lap quietly as Jesse and I talked to their mother and as the large, gregarious woman braided her older daughter's thick and shiny hair, worked it into manageable shapes secured by strings and ribbons and bobby pins.

A few blocks from home, my phone rang again, and this time it was Katie's father who, though he didn't live in the house, played an active role in his children's lives. He was polite but firm, stating that "black hair is different," and I interrupted begging forgiveness, and assuring him that I understand that it is different from most "white hair," and that I was very, very wrong to allow Annie to play with Katie's hair, and that I hoped he and Katie's mother would trust me to monitor the girls better next time.

Whereas, with the exception of two or three genuine friendships growing up, I have learned and internalized the bleak history of race relations in America mostly at a distance, Annie is learning and internalizing that history in close proximity. When she learns how many thousands of lynchings occurred in America between, say, 1870 and 1940, that knowledge will be attached to innumerable images of happy, affluent African-American families lovingly joking with one another, living fun lives, and by images of beautiful young black men and women celebrating their sexuality unabashedly. When she reads accounts of what happened to men of color who expressed any sexual attraction to white women, how whole communities of white people would participate in the slow torture and murder of men of color accused, often on the shoddiest of evidence, of raping white women, that knowledge will be dovetailed with her own unashamed sexual attraction to beautiful "dark" men and/or women.

Will the horror of such knowledge be even more resonant for her than it was for me? Or will the proximity fostered by a multicultural school system reinforced, albeit insipidly, by the media, create the opposite effect? In other words, will she as a consequence be emotionally numb? When she tries to fathom, for example, the implications of so many African-American men being incarcerated in America, how will Raven or Will Smith (during her Disney phase she also loved re-runs of *The Fresh Prince of Bel-Air*), mediate her contemplation?

Because of her cultural conditioning regarding race, it may be that she does not "other" African-Americans, and non-European-Americans generally, as distinctly, on a deep psychological level, as European-Americans of my generation and older most assuredly do.

I recall the segregated South, the "negro" high school playing its games some Friday nights in Elizabeth City, North Carolina, and the white high school on other Friday nights. That late spring of 1961, my father was caught by the highway patrol somewhere in central Florida, and my mother called her mother, who lived in Elizabeth City, for bus fare.

After months of crowding a great-aunt's humble bungalow, we got on welfare and moved into the second-floor apartment of a battered house whose downstairs occupants kept a goat in the backyard. It was the very first house occupied by white people; for many blocks beyond it, the exclusively black section of town sprawled. From the southern window of that apartment I could gaze onto the high school football field that was adjacent not to either the white or black high schools, but to the white elementary school I attended. I thrilled to the white high school games: the lights; the packed bleachers; gangs of prepubescents playing "Smear the Queer" on the sidelines with balled-up paper cups for a ball (you were a queer when you caught the wad and had to run around without any boundaries or goal until you got tackled and everyone piled on top of you); trolling under the bleachers for loose change and empty bottles to cash in for one, two, or three cents depending upon which grocery store you took them to (alas, one cent was close, two cents three or four blocks away, and three cents a forbidding half mile). But on those Fridays when the black high school played an out-of-town black opponent, I could only watch from my high window as the—not marching but—dancing band, so much better than the white one, so much more musically interesting and kinetic, so much more fun, entered the gate onto the field, and the bleachers filled with dark people. I could see the game when it was between the twenties, but could not for the angles see the teams play in the red zones, so could gauge scores only by the sound of the crowd and the band. It never crossed my mind to go down to the gate and walk through, join their version of "Smear the Queer" or whatever they called it (no one whom I can recall defined "queer" as anyone but the kid who ran around until he got tackled; we all got to be queer once or twice over the course of that exhilaratingly pointless, scoreless game), or simply sit in the bleachers and watch. I was seven, eight, and nine; the separation, in my heart, was absolute. My fatherless family lived on the border between two kinds of people, light and dark, and the two never played together, never even spoke much. We left each other alone.

When I learned history a few years later, especially about the Civil War, I got the sanitized Great Man stuff they taught back then, and of course as a young man devouring (mostly leftist) social theory and history, I perceived everything in terms of social justice, and the strange fruit Lady Day sang about was very, very dark indeed. He was something like a pure victim, and so I did not identify with him. He was so dark, so other, so victimized, that I could rarely see him as anything but symbol, and so I could not feel his humanity. On a very basic level, I could not empathize. I could shudder at the abstract knowledge of his terror and pain; I could cry out against his victimization, and the wretched social system that victimized him, but I don't recall wincing in discomfort imagining what it must have felt like to be set upon by an entire community, then to be hanged by the neck and set on fire as light-skinned men, women, and children laughed and cheered.

Empathy is, in some part, a conditioned response, and entails a readiness, at least a willingness, to identify with someone or something. Social justice in the abstract is like the idea of a six-course gourmet meal; in the abstract, nothing sustains. When that plucky teen Raven was in the throes of yet another vision of the near future that that chunky, cute young woman would misinterpret to hilarious effect (hilarious if you're a nine-year-old transfixed by such affable misprision and high jinx), Annie deeply identified with the character. She, Annie Katrovas, wanted to have visions of the near future and daily misadventures. She wanted to have friends like Raven's friends, go to a school like Raven's school, even have parents like Raven's, parents who weren't divorced. She wanted a home like Raven's, in a "neighborhood," not a downtown condo in America for half the year and an apartment in Central Europe for the other. She was then, and still is, a happy, tough, well-adjusted, deeply loving, and lovable kid, but back then, when she was nine, before she blossomed into the five-foot nine, drop-dead beautiful teenager she's become, she would have traded her life in a second for Raven's. Annie *would have been* Raven if the universe had allowed her to be, and she would have been Beyoncé. For a time, at least, she would have been any beautiful, successful, glamorous American woman of color.

In light of such uninhibited identification, what then will she see when she reads eyewitness accounts of lynchings? How will she imagine herself into the scene? Certainly not as a member of the pale mob. Will she imagine herself into the skin of the dark-skinned person gagging at the end of a rope and feeling the flames take and rise? Will her conscience, the pituitary of social justice, flood her being with outrage? Or will she, simply and profoundly, feel empathy? Outrage and empathy are not, of course, mutually exclusive; indeed, only when outrage is derived from empathy is a true moral imperative created, that is, not one fostered by abstract logic alone but born of the beating heart of a man or a woman.

I return often to the memory of one spring in Elizabeth City, when I was eight or nine. I heard a boy younger than I (it appeared from his stature) but possessing a preternaturally deep and shat-tered voice, screaming at dawn on consecutive mornings, though I can't recall how many—it now seems the entire season—"Richard, Richard Lee! Richard, Richard Lee!" over and over, weeping, sometimes literally naked in the fog or gloom, some-times wearing drawers. Hours earlier than I was to rise for school, I peered over the windowsill down at him, and was terrified. He came from the heart of the black section of town. He stumbled, wept, and cried that name, though the first time he awoke me I thought he was saying, "Richard, Richard leave! Richard, Richard leave!" I thought that for some reason he wanted me gone.

There was a rumor among the whites in my neighborhood that the boy was a sleepwalker; Richard Lee was his brother who'd been stabbed to death down by the tracks, that the ghostly boy wept his brother's name every morning, right up to the edge of Merrimac Street, parallel to my house, then turned and stumbled back, weeping, rasping that name. Cecil Hooker said the boy walked back into his house, lay back down, then woke up a few hours later and acted normal, went to school and everything. It was not at all likely that Cecil Hooker, whose younger brother Jigger was my best friend, would have possessed reliable information about the child, but he was the only source of information, dubious though it may have been.

Whatever his story, he was a child in deepest distress. He keened to the edge of his world, then retreated, still keening. He loved another human being, a man or boy named Richard Lee, very much. He wanted to see and touch Richard Lee, hear his voice. I was terrified of that child, how he made me feel. I missed my father. I'd never lived in one place before, so I missed my life with my family on the road, in cars, sleeping in the rear window-space of a Chrysler with my father's aftershave-tainted jacket over me, my siblings rasping on the seat below, or in a motel after a score, a bounced check for clean sheets and a TV.

The child was fixity, the particular voice of a particular place. He was life's circuit, a going forth in utter sadness and returning likewise. He was no escape. He was everybody knowing my father was in prison. He was my weeping, distracted mother, or, rather, he was her weeping and distraction. He was the leak in our roof and the urine-stinking sheets of my siblings. He was that evil goat.

He was every vexation, the bat that whacked fourteen stitches in my forehead and the blood that poured down my throat from a botched tonsillectomy.

The question of how a five- or six-year-old child could rise from sleep, presumably leave his domicile on many consecutive mornings and wander up and down the street rasping a name, is now overshadowed by the question of why no one, no adult, black or white, intervened, at least none of which I'm aware.

In this regard, I can only speak, albeit unreliably given how much time has passed, for my side of the divide. My own young mother, twenty-seven or eight, wondered aloud many times about his circumstance but never thought to walk down our rickety steps and into the dawn-glazed street to intervene. Everyone in that white neighborhood, toward the official end of the era of segregation, talked about the boy that season. I heard friends' parents mention him, chuckling and shaking their heads, and, of course, the kids speculated wildly about the boy, but no one thought to intervene. A child was so clearly distressed, so unambiguously in need of succor, and it now seems that no one was capable of even imagining the simple act of approaching him, much less holding him.

Solidarity

ALL POLITICS IS LOCAL, AND ALL talk about it small and mean. Somewhere between Self Interest and the Good of the Many, most noble intentions get scrubbed of nobility.

I recently received a mass e-mail from the local chapter of my union imploring my colleagues and me to show "solidarity" with striking food workers on campus by boycotting graduation ceremonies. My first impulse was positive, though that quickly dissolved into incredulity. I'm a college teacher. Notwithstanding the fact that I was a janitor, dishwasher, cook, busboy, and waiter in more than a dozen restaurants through my youth, do I have any right to feel "solidarity" with food workers?

The American Association of University Professors was conceived to protect tenure and therefore the principle of academic freedom; I'm fairly certain it wasn't meant at its inception to be an agent for collective bargaining, and therefore to engage in all the complex and petty political machinations that that implies, indeed necessitates. The fact that it has become primarily a bargaining agent, at least in union-randy Michigan, should not be surprising. American universities almost always reflect the ethos of the states in which they were conceived. In Michigan, AAUP has simply morphed into something resembling the UAW; and the relations, therefore, between university administrators ("management") and the professorate ("the workers") play out accordingly. However, I believe, though with little passion, that AAUP should be more a professional organization along the lines of the ABA or AMA than an agent for collective bargaining. I think, too, that university professors indulging in the traditional rhetoric of labor unions is silly. Unless we're willing to advocate for a tenure system for university support staff, our "solidarity" with food workers is self-serving and hollow; besides, tenure as such is only justifiable relative to issues of academic freedom. I certainly support the idea and practice of collective bargaining in all fields; I'm just not certain that professional associations are the appropriate agents for such bargaining. Hearing me discuss this issue recently with a friend and colleague, Annie asked me flat out what a union is. I explained. She was taken with the term "labor organizer." She asked if I've ever been a labor organizer. Once I tried to be one, I answered.

Louisiana is the antithesis of Michigan in its historic relation to labor unions. The union at the university where I taught in New Orleans for twenty years was weak, largely ineffectual. I joined it for a while out of a sentimental attachment to the idea of unions. A "right to work" state, Louisiana, for all its Huey Long egalitarianism, is salted soil for organized labor. The ethos of Louisiana politics is such that the networks of ensconced local pols, crafty disseminators of largess, serve the function of "protecting" workers. This paternalistic mindset, which places the conduct of grassroots politics between, in the sense of a partition, workers and owners seems often to serve the interests of the latter at least as often as it does the former, yet one hears little grousing from working people in the state, and the same rascals, and their progeny, get reelected again and again, though one can only hope that Katrina has broken the cycle.

I got it in my head one spring, as I was working in a fancy French Quarter restaurant while on hiatus from graduate school, to organize the waiters into a union. I was in my mid twenties, frisky and mischievous; I knew that my time in that world was limited, that I'd likely get a job in academe in a couple of years, though I had no idea I'd find a position in New Orleans. I was certain that fairly soon the Big Easy would be in my past, so I had nothing to lose stirring up a little labor strife within the community of itinerants who worked the city's storied restaurants, the people who hustled in one establishment for a year or two, or just a few months, got fired for thievery or insubordination, moved on to another restaurant with similar results, only to end up back at the scene of the original crime.

"Consider the spirit of the Poles!" I remember declaiming in the Bienville Room, the darkened banquet space where six or seven of us sat folding napkins by candlelight and shooting the breeze before the first customers got seated.

"Poles ain't got no spirit," Malcolm breathed, bored, only half listening.

"I mean the Poles in Poland," I clarified. Malcolm flicked his eyes up, gave me a look that said he was certain Poles everywhere lack any vestige of the Holy Ghost. But I was undaunted. The guys loved it when I was on a roll, indulging in a mock pedantry they could goof on.

"Solidarity!" I yelled. "We must organize in the spirit of Solidarity!"

"We organized," Buddy, a proud "coonass," the oddly non-derogatory nickname for Cajuns, said, then wiggled the tip of his tongue into the fold of his napkin, a tired joke; triangulated, they looked like female genitalia. "I got my section set up, you got yours. We organized."

"Gentlemen, the maître d' rips us off for a third of our tips. We get paid next to nothing by the restaurant. We work the hours and days we're told with no overtime. We get fired on a whim. We have no healthcare coverage. We're slaves!"

"I don't wanna hear no honky sayin' he a slave," said TJ. "My great-granddaddy, he was a slave, and your great-granddaddy probably kick his chained-up ass. I should just kick yo ass right here!"

Hearty laughs all around.

"Gentlemen, this is a serious matter." All of them balled up napkins and pelted me. "We are the wretched of the earth! We are the victims of unabashed exploitation!"

More balled-up napkins. The nub of an unlit candle. "Burt, how long have you been working here?" Burt was at least sixty, and one of the only waiters I'd ever met who'd remained for an entire career at one establishment.

"Since I was humpin' yo mama," he growled, not looking up from his pile of folded linen, and everybody cheered. "Yo grandma, too," he added, perfectly timed.

"Billy, when you tripped over that crate in the walk-in and busted your nose, what did the restaurant do for you?"

"They didn't fire me. I was in there smoking a joint." Everyone nodded his head knowingly. Everyone knew you weren't supposed to smoke dope in the walk-in.

"Did they pay your hospital bill? Did they give you sick pay?"

"What's sick pay?" Elvis asked earnestly. His name was Dante, but TJ said he looked like his sister's dog, named Elvis.

"It's when you get paid for being sick," Buster informed him.

"Shit," Elvis breathed, truly perplexed. "Like when you sell blood?"

No one got the connection, but Elvis was special that way.

"It's when you get compensated even when you're sick and can't work," I said.

"Dick," Burt said, knowing how I hated to be called that, "You gonna get shot in the head." He lit a cigarette and watched the smoke rise. Our tuxes shone a little in the candlelight; our bow ties dangled, clipped to shirt collars, but not Burt's. He wore an old-fashioned tie and he actually manipulated it into a perfect bow before the mirror in the employee room.

I was a little startled. "Why?"

"Talking that shit, boy. Somebody's gonna come up behind you and bust a cap in yo cerebellum." Burt was a smart man who could use big words for effect.

"Who?" I asked.

"Oh, just about anybody. You fucking with the status quo, boy, talking that organized labor bullshit."

Of course, much of this is reconstruction; I can't recall verbatim what was said that day in March, I think, right before or after Mardi Gras. It was a nice day, in the low seventies; I remember the blue skies and balmy air because earlier that day I'd taken a long, memorable walk from the Quarter where I lived and worked all the way up St. Charles to the end, to Carrollton, then rode the streetcar back to Canal. I smoked back then; I'd smoke a whole pack on long walks like that; I smoked and strode taking it all in, that incredible city of gross inequities and graceful ignorance, a city steeped in a civic narcissism so profound its poorest citizens feel privileged to occupy it. It's a beautiful place, more soulfully beautiful even than its hype suggests. From the inside, it's a place hard to imagine leaving.

"Yeah, what are you, Dick, one of them outside agitators?" said Jose. Jose was brilliant, a real Marxist who could talk the talk. He read Spanish poetry in Spanish and thought Trotsky got what he deserved. He found me amusing. No one else, except maybe Burt, got the "outside agitator" joke.

"Surely *you* support organizing the workers!" I said, trying not to seem shaken by Burt's warning.

Jose just smiled. He wasn't even going to bother. He chugged some ice water, chewed a cube.

"Well, shit," said Elvis. This I recall vividly because of what followed: "Sounds like a good idea to me."

"Yeah, maybe," Malcolm said, though I knew he just liked the idea of me getting shot in the head, or at least worrying about it. "How do we get started?" he said. "I want some of that sick pay. Overtime, too."

"Really, Burt, who'd want to shoot me in the head? Mafia?"

Burt chuckled slow and wicked, blew some little rings through a big one. He was an older man with lots of tricks. "Mafia don't give a shit. Mafia likes unions. Take 'em over in no time."

"So who'd shoot me?"

He blew three rapid rings through a bigger one, stared off. His silence was pregnant with my doom.

"So let's get started on this union," said TJ, enjoying my discomfort enormously. He winked at Jose, who crunched another cube.

"First thing you've got to do," said Jose, "is call a meeting. You've got to get a space, then put out the word, make some nice fliers. Hardly anybody'll come the first time. But you've got to keep having meetings. The numbers will grow over the weeks, months, right up to when you get shot in the head," he finished, and the guys cracked up. "Then everybody'll act like you never existed, and like they never heard of any union." Burt, especially, liked the way Jose put it.

"Yeah, you right," he chuckled. "See, Dick, what we got here, in this room, in this restaurant, all over the Quarter, is some serious solidarity." He and Jose did whatever sequence of fist-knocks was in fashion that year.

"But don't you feel exploited?" I said weakly. "I mean, do you want to continue giving the Fat Man a third of your tips?" The Fat Man was the maître d' who was evil but loveably so.

Of course, no one felt exploited. The Fat Man took care of the guys who took care of him; he and Burt were old buds; Burt had worked there through five or six maître d's, would outlast this one, and he'd get the same deal from the next one as he got with all of them: he walked with at least a hundred bucks every night, no matter what, even in bumfuck August. Sometimes he'd walk with three hundred; for working the all-nighters in the banquet room when the four Arabs, we called them "the princes," each brought two hookers and spent the equivalent of a mid-range automobile, I'd get a hundred, Burt'd get two even though I was expected to do all the heavy lifting, and the maître d', one of whose seven languages was Arabic, split a thousand sixty/forty with the chef. Even Elvis, who worked there as a favor to his uncle—a beloved bookie—poor dim Elvis, working a little station of three deuces, walked most nights with fifty. In the high season I always walked with at least a hundred, and rarely, even in bumfuck August, walked with less than forty.

Burt had a fancy shoeshine stand in one of the other glitzy hotels; he ran it with his two sons and they made a killing, he assured me. The maître d' ran an escort service with his wife who was a concierge in one of the other hotels, though not the one where Burt shined shoes. Malcolm played jazz piano well enough to make a living. Buddy worked on his daddy's shrimp boat during the season, and would someday inherit it. TJ wanted to go to barber school, open his own shop; meanwhile, on the side he was a runner for the maître d's escort business. Jose would work through his youth in French Quarter restaurants, moving from one to the next. On a steamy morning more than twenty years later, while jogging in a part of Mid-City that would soon be destroyed by Katrina, I'd watch him get arrested in his tuxedo, though I'd never know for what. Billy would die of an overdose in two or three months; the maître d' would move me to his larger station. Elvis would be taken in by a rich man, become a kind of uptown housewife; I'd see him and his benefactor shopping in Whole Foods years later, knocking on melons, squeezing avocados.

Destiny is the organizing principle under which all others are subsumed, made petty. In a dark room, a candlelit moment of my late youth, among men I did not know but for our common purpose and the emotional truths we could massage from the lies we'd tell one another, the boasts and subterfuge behind which our uncertainties and self-loathing huddled, there was a solidarity born of our common disregard for one another, our sense that we were all of us waiting for something, something else.

Not America

BEFORE MY FATHER WENT TO FEDERAL prison the first time, as we traversed the North American continent in a series of automobiles my father acquired illegally for the sole purpose of transporting a family of three, four, five, six, and finally seven from one illegal transaction to the next, he would have to lie low once in a while. The first time he took us off the road for a few weeks we stayed in Montreal. It was 1959. I was six, so my father decided I should start school, even though he knew we would only be at that location for three to five weeks, and even though he knew, I assume, that the school I'd attend would most likely be conducted in French.

He enrolled me, using, of course, false documents, in a private Catholic school, which he surely paid with a bad check, for kiting checks was his métier. He hired a twelve-year-old boy who spoke a little English, lived close to us, and attended that school, to walk me there and back.

I was yelled at, scorned by a teacher who was disgusted that I could not speak or understand French. I was stashed in a corner, facing a wall, given French-language textbooks, and left there all day. As miserable as life on the road, cooped up in the backseats of innumerable cars with younger siblings, could be, I'd never known, in some respects would never know again, such misery, such humiliation. I recall that teacher, a bald man who seemed to take his job very seriously, yelling at me for minutes at a time as though comprehension might suddenly click if only he scared me sufficiently. After a couple of weeks (probably about the same time it became apparent to the school bursar that the check from Florida, Utah, or Colorado would not clear), my father packed us up and drove us away to resume our criminal regimen in the Lower Forty-eight. I recall the relief I felt when my father assured me I'd not have to go back to that terrible place where I was hated, where all the boys laughed at me, tormented me, and where that bald teacher spat all over me when he screamed in my face.

Just as I will always be the son of a convicted felon, so my children will always be the daughters of an American poet (or ex-poet, as I now present myself). In some respects, they have no less to live down than I, though they may come to a similar conclusion that, contrary to ancient opinion, a father's sins needn't be visited upon subsequent generations.

My crazy young father was indifferent to learning, and conceived the life of the mind in terms of stretches of quiet road when we kids were in a long-distance stupor, or sleeping. My crazy young mother was a dreamer, though I cannot presume to know what she dreamed riding shotgun to my father for so many years of small felonies and stealthy getaways.

I attended roughly four years total of my first seven years of school; my formal learning was uninterrupted only those years my father was incarcerated. My daughters' lives between two continents, two cultures, two languages, are no less unsettled and unsettling than the life I knew as a child, though their lives are unambiguously privileged whereas mine was underprivileged in certain obvious ways, though quite privileged, if ambiguously so, from my present perspective. Indeed, my "present perspective" is as much a matter of my peering out from a weird childhood as it is a function of enculturation, and so it will be for my girls.

In school, from the very beginning, I felt unique, but only because I knew that no one else around me lived the way my family did. In other environs of the "underprivileged," there is usually a range of shared circumstances; in the government housing projects where we lived the second time my father went to prison, there were probably other kids whose fathers were "away learning a trade," as I was taught to say, but I didn't know any. In the early and mid-sixties, the projects (at least the facility in Norfolk, Virginia, we inhabited) were bi-racial if segregated, and the ethos of the community centered on the assumption that one occupied the projects until one's circumstances changed for the better, and moving up and out was possible. The projects were not a ghetto in the sense of a permanent community determined by severe limitations and despair, at least for those of us living at the "white" end; I will not presume to speak for our black neighbors, though my strong intuition is that the hope bubbling out of the Civil Rights Movement surely spilled among them. The fact of the matter is that I felt unique among the underprivileged if only because the first seven years of my life had been in cars, on the road, hiding from authorities. Somehow, my parents had communicated that we were hiding, that we were outlaws but that we were good and the police were bad. Every time we drove through a city or town, we kids were tense because our parents were. We learned to duck down to confound head-counts, because of course the authorities knew our number. By the time our father got out of prison the first time, five-to-ten-out-in-three, and he started the whole process yet again, the five of us kids were old enough to understand just how odd was our life on the road, if only because we'd spent three "normal" years living in one place, attending school, eating every day.

This is all to say that I understand my daughters when they express their sense of being, certainly not superior, but unique among their peers in both countries. No one they know lives the way they do, alternating schools on two continents; calling two abodes, thousands of miles apart, home; racking up more frequent-flier miles than many grizzled business mavens.

Both of my school-age daughters speak often of the differences between the two school systems, the two school cultures. One big difference is that whereas all of their Czech peers are profoundly aware of American popular culture, hardly any of their American teachers, much less their peers, are aware of any discrete aspect of Czech culture and history. In Czech schools, they are "othered" as Americans, though no one knows that they are American until that bit of information is transmitted in the course of daily exchange, for example when some of their friends hear them talking to me as I pick them up from school. In America, they are othered only to the extent that I make their being Czech an issue to teachers, explaining at the beginning of first grade, for example, that Annie didn't attend kindergarten because the Czech public school system (a few years ago ranked behind only Singapore's in math and science) simply doesn't have it, and explaining to Ema's eighth and then ninth-grade English teachers that though she's broadly read, relatively speaking, in two literatures, and though she writes, relatively speaking, quite beautifully in both languages, they should be patient with her spelling regarding in-class assignments; Czech spelling is consistently phonetic, and of course English spelling is insane. My daughters' American teachers have been understanding, accommodating in response to my gentle pleas of special circumstances, as have been their Czech teachers: however, the latter have been less so if only because they assume their system to be the far superior one. A couple of my daughters' Czech teachers have seemed to assume that my girls' education in America is more or less a waste of time, a disadvantage I impose upon them.

When she was in the fourth grade, Ema one day found a school lunch offering odious and refused to eat it. The attending teacher scoffed, "Maybe in America you can eat all the hamburgers you want, but . . ." What followed didn't matter. The public stereotyping had occurred. It was innocuous, but symptomatic of the unique social context Ema has had to learn to negotiate. In Prague, she will always be the American girl who speaks perfect Czech but who hauls within her all the sins of her American father, which is to say all the sins of a superpower by turns nefarious and magnanimous.

The most corrosive feature of stereotypes is that they disallow complexity; however, reductions akin to stereotypes are to be expected. For example, social scientists generalize about behavior from statistics; economists collect data to deduce a typical consumer. A stereotype is a cruder version of the same impulse.

Perhaps the most vexing stereotype my daughters face in Prague schools is that American public education is generally bad, too easy, too coddling. The fact of the matter is that no nation on earth has attempted to educate a population so large *and* so diverse. There are public schools in America, and probably thousands of them, that are as good as any in the world. There are some that are among the worst, too, doubtless an equal number. Even the "average" public high school may be so only because its pockets of excellence are cancelled out by its zones of failure, alas too often along racial and class lines.

In recent years, an inordinate number of Gypsy ("Roma") kids have been labeled retarded simply because they couldn't conform to the Czech system of education, and because that system is frankly racist. The Czechs, like all of Europe, largely conflate national identity and ethnicity, and being a largely homogenous population (the difference between Bohemians and Moravians is quaint even to the two groups), they accommodate the contemporary Other—Gypsies, Vietnamese, Slavs from farther east, and Americans—in fashion similar to the way Jews were once received, with mild condescension that can turn very ugly in a crisis. The Czechs are notorious xenophobes, and, of course, in stating this I'm perpetuating a stereotype. One must, moreover, acknowledge a distinction between the xenophobia of a small nation, a relatively tiny language group that has been overrun, indeed, devastated by larger powers for a thousand years, and the xenophobia of a continent-size nation bordered by oceans.

Our present situation regarding the girls' schooling is crazy but, so far, working. Our divorce settlement has the girls with me in the fall, but winter through spring in Prague. I'm in Prague through the summer, and live in an apartment in the building my ex-wife owns and where she and the girls reside on another floor. Our daughters shuttle between the two spaces throughout the summer.

Ema, seventeen, is a junior double-majoring in music and english at Western Michigan University, so far carrying a 3.9 GPA. Much to her mother's chagrin, and at my insistence, she left the Czech public school system in the eighth grade, having to that point attended school in Prague for five years. It was my contention that, given that she would attend college in the United States, she should, through middle and high school, be immersed in English. After the divorce, to comply with the custody agreement, Ema, while still a high school student, took college courses at Western Michigan University within a special program that allowed her to do so, and then in the spring studied in a Charles University exchange program primarily for American students. When she reached a point where she was technically a high-school senior who would not be able to graduate because she could not attend her final semester, and yet had accrued enough college credits to have sophomore university status, she simply got an online diploma and is continuing into her junior year at WMU.

She's taken an odd route, but, from my point of view, an effective one. Annie, eleven, is taking an even odder route; she's attending public school in Kalamazoo in the fall, then in Prague in the winter and spring. The last two school cycles, fourth and fifth grade, have been split. She's a fiercely bright kid, socially adept, effervescent, verbally dexterous, a wonderful arguer, not swift with numbers but not terrible. Both her schools have been very cooperative, but surely there will be a point at which this will cease to work. And what are we to do about the baby? I insist that she should attend day care and kindergarten, the first half, at least, in Kalamazoo; her mother will dig in her heels at some point, sooner rather than later.

What are we to do? I don't want my girls not to be educated in English. Dominika doesn't want them not to be educated in Czech. She feels that the allure of American popular culture gives me an unfair advantage, and, yes, we both feel in competition with the other, though we are trying to see beyond that feeling to what is best for our girls.

But what is best? Are we faced with a Solomon-like decision? Ema's case is settled. Annie will have quite a bit of say as to how we'll proceed regarding her education. And what are we to do with Ellie? Dominika is set upon her being primarily Czech, secondarily American. She feels that I have won with the older two, that I somehow owe her this one. But I love that child no less than I love Ema and Annie. I would be profoundly sad if she were in any way foreign to me, and I know that Ema and Annie are not foreign to their mother. It's just that what's American in them in subtle ways overwhelms what is Czech.

One cannot know, truly, what it is to be American until one has achieved some form of intimacy with what is not American. Intimacy is knowledge. It is knowing private, daily habits and how they are determined by a shared, public identity. Dominika will always be my measure of what is not American, and so, the divorce notwithstanding, she determines my identity as an American. How we negotiate, between ourselves and our girls, what of our daughters will be American and what not American is also a larger negotiation between our two cultures. Part of who and what my ex-wife is issues back over a thousand years. A deeply intelligent, gifted person, she carries in her heart the (losing) Battle of White Mountain and (betrayed) Jan Hus burning at the stake. She holds in her heart every novel Kundera composed in Czech, and a simmering resentment at those not. She holds most dearly the Bohemian countryside, memories of dead grandparents. She loves what she is as I may never love what I am. America is too big for me to love. It is too big, in its physical and metaphysical entirety, to be home. Only pieces of it can be home, only aspects. But Dominika's Not America, her homeland, Bohemia, the Czech Republic, may be traversed from any point of the compass in a few hours. It is ancient, well defined, knowable. It is what she wants to give our daughters, and I want mightily for them to have it, but I have feared, and still fear, that that part of them that is Not American, is Bohemian, may overwhelm what is American if I don't press my cause. As Czech-Americans, as culturally and linguistically hyphenated beings, they are a new kind of citizen of the world, one that could not have existed before 1989 and one more valuable, ironically, to their motherland than to their fatherland. Their skills in and with the *lingua franca* render them more valuable in the Czech Republic than their knowledge of Czech could ever be in America. Schools are, perhaps above all else, crucibles of acculturation. They finish the job of building cultural identity that begins in the family. Through our girls a tiny, ancient place at the heart of Europe is tethered to a protean behemoth, a beast in whose belly I am at home.

SOMETIMES, AFTER A MEAL OF BURGERS passed from a bag to the backseat, as the sun was setting into a cornfield or ocean or distant mountain, my first family would sing together. The sepia light fading, the wind waffling through windows cranked down halfway, the glow of the speedometer misting my young father's arms, he would begin "Home on the Range" or "You Are My Sunshine" or "Lovesick Blues," and my mother would chime in, and then I and my brothers and sister would, and even the youngest would croon along, and we'd sing the same chorus again and again until the youngest fell asleep, and as the singing faded to humming to quiet, all the children but me would be asleep, and I'd lean my head upon the front seat and dream of a home I'd never known, of something like I'd see on TV in motels, the domesticated nuclear family being funny and tender, oblivious to everything but its own charmed circumstances.

I didn't know that I was at home in transit. I didn't know that America was right there, and would always be right there.

Going Native

My Czech ex-wife does not particularly enjoy her brief stays in Kalamazoo, Michigan, to visit our daughters in the fall, but she primarily doesn't like being away from her work in Prague for more than a few days at a time. She is a freelance interpreter/translator, and since the Czech Republic joined the European Union, she has been commuting a lot between Prague and Brussels, though there is plenty of work for her in Prague. The only problem is that if she is out of the loop for more than a couple of weeks, she finds herself, upon returning to Prague, having painstakingly to reestablish contacts it has taken her years to build. Couple this with the fact that our teenage daughter is no longer shuttling between the Czech and US school systems but is now exclusively pursuing English-language education in the States (much to her mother's chagrin); and the fact that our second daughter will, as did her sister, alternate between the two school systems for a number of years we're still negotiating; and the fact that we now have a toddler third daughter, and it should be obvious to anyone that the "Katrovas/Winterová experiment," as the fabulous Czech poet Pavel Šrut once dubbed our family, could at any moment blow up and wreck the lab.

I am lucky to have a job that allows me to do all my teaching in the fall semester and be off in the spring to write and to mount a summer program for my university. However, even though I am blessed with such a flexible job, my ex-wife and I continue to confront the problem, as parenting partners now if not as mates, that shattered our marriage: She can never feel herself anything but a visitor in America, and I likewise in the Czech Republic. We can never feel at home in the other's country. Neither of us was constitutionally capable of "going native" as the old, vaguely condescending and imperialist term used to designate cultural assimilation. Dominika's incredible facility with English means that assimilation to American culture for her could be literally an overnight occurrence, an unconscious event, even, but this suggests that her not assimilating has been an act of will, a conscious decision, a political act of good faith with who and what she is.

We are quite decent to each other regarding this problem, but are beginning to experience considerable anxiety about the future. Our baby daughter was a joyful accident. At my present age of fifty-three, I experience anxiety about being appropriately present in her life even under optimal circumstances. But I know that into my sixties she will have to shuttle, as have Ema and Annie, between America and Central Europe if she is to achieve the bilingual, bi-cultural psyche that has already coalesced in her sisters; otherwise, she will be—and I have feared this mightily regarding my two older daughters and, happily, have been spared the circumstance—a native-speaking Czech for whom English is a second, not co-equal, language. If this happens, she and I will consequently be, always, just a little foreign to one another. She will also feel a little foreign in relation to her sisters, at least the American part of them, in similar fashion to how I seem foreign to Dominika, and she to me.

If I'd gone native, what would have happened in a few years when my daughters attend college in America, as they almost certainly will (Ema has already, technically, completed her sophomore year at my university)? If I'd had the courage to go native, retire, and live exclusively in Prague, what would anchor them to America? How could they make lives in America with no local family support? It seems quite likely that the two older ones will want to work and live at least partly in the United States, where their mother will never live and where I could not if I were to remain in anything like a marriage with her, and therefore our marriage has to become something else, a parenting alliance of some sort, certainly a friendship, but not a marriage as most Czechs and Americans consider that primal relationship.

Of course, we are blessed. We are proud of the lives we have thus far been able to fashion for our girls, and enjoy our continent-hopping lifestyle. It has simply dawned on us that though we are friends, committed parenting partners, faithful and successful colleagues, we have evolved into something other than a married couple, if indeed two people maintaining primary abodes on separate continents precludes a relationship most thoughtful folks would consider a legitimate marriage. We confront the same mid-life exigencies as other long-married couples, the quotidian nuisances the cumulative weight of which rip open half of all marriages in both our countries, but the spatial relations of our union on the one hand affords us a sobering perspective on the quotidian, and on the other exacerbates the usual processes by which a couple's problems get solved. We are so used to being apart—sometimes divided by an ocean, though just as often, in both countries, when Dominika is off on a job and I am single parenting, or when the girls are with her and I am teaching, or one of our daughters is with me and the other with her for two or three weeks in the transition from one continent to the other—that we can usually simply wait out domestic tensions, thus avoiding crises.

But such a condition is itself a permanent crisis. I confess this dilemma with neither shame nor sadness, and would only state it so publicly after many months of calm and deliberate discussion with Dominika. We've come to the conclusion that the one aspect of marriage we are not able to negotiate is a quality of companionship that requires the more or less constant vigilance that only more or less constant presence will allow, that only a constantly shared home life will allow.

And can that be managed as long as her home is on one continent and mine on another, as long as we continue to be visitors in each other's homes, aliens in each other's countries?

If we cared for one another in the manner we would like to be cared for at this stage of our lives, I would be arguing that it should be I who goes native in Bohemia, and she would be saying no, it is she who should go native in America, but the unvarnished fact is that neither of us can do it; we can continue visiting the other's home, and probably will, for many years, but we are quite certain that we simply will not, either of us, go native.

Over the years I've met numerous Americans who have sought to assimilate into Czech culture and society. Of course, the first prerequisite is learning the language beyond mere survival competence, which is to say far beyond the level I have achieved. There is a woman who came to Prague at about the same time as I, on a Fulbright, already possessing some classroom knowledge of Czech; she and her American companion live the bohemian life in Bohemia, teaching English and working with social justice NGOs. She has not gone native even though she has become fluent in Czech; this is primarily because she hates Czech society only a little less than she hates American society. She and her companion are poets who network within the sprawled community of social activist-artist types who are the cornerstone of the Central European expatriate community, a tribe scattered primarily between Berlin, Prague, Warsaw, and Budapest. They represent an ironic feature of American cultural imperialism: unreconstructed lefties who deign to live off local economies (usually teaching English) and to instruct the natives on such issues as Gypsy rights, assuming, I suppose, that the job of eradicating racism in America has been completed.

But there is also the terrific Irish poet and critic Justin Quinn, who married a Czech, became fluent in Czech, indeed translates Czech poetry quite proficiently. He teaches at Charles University where there are numerous aficionados of Irish literature and culture. It seems there is a delightfully odd atavistic connection between the Irish and Czechs inasmuch as the latter claim Celtic origins by virtue of numerous prehistoric Celtic settlements having been excavated in Bohemia. Be that as it may, there is also the more resonant connection between two tiny nations whose identities have been determined by their constantly having to fend off the hegemony of historical oppressors. Quinn has achieved an enviable grace in his Bohemian life. He has not exactly gone native, it seems, remaining vitally connected to the Irish/British

literary scene as a poet, critic, and editor; as a translator and edu-
cator he's become an important conduit, too, between the literary
cultures of two small though vital literary communities. He
seems to be living a life wholly in good faith with his host culture, his Czech wife and young Irish-Czech son.

But the American social activists and Irish poet occupy a zone
of engagement between the classic expatriate and the assimilated
foreigner. The individuals I've met who have gone native have
immersed themselves in the culture. They are almost always
women who have married, or at one time were deeply involved
with, Czech men. With the exception of one, they have not
seemed in any sense extraordinary. They have harbored no literary ambitions I could discern, have not been moved to write
memoirs recounting the process of assimilation. The one who did
seem extraordinary had been involved with a semi-famous Czech
writer who dumped her. I chatted with her at a literary event held
in the US ambassador's residence. She expressed cosmic resentment toward the semi-famous writer, but credited the relationship with facilitating her fluency in Czech. She owns her own
company, her own flat, hates George Bush's America, is an inde-
pendent American woman who is committed to living the rest of
her life in the Czech Republic. She derives all of her news of the
world from the Czech press, and seems to have little tolerance for
fellow Americans, such as myself, who occupy Bohemia in
English-language and American-culture bubbles; I did not resent
her mild condescension because she'd so clearly earned it. But
she, too, by virtue of her exquisite independence, and by virtue of
the fact that her business involves interacting with English-
language book publishers, is mediated in her relation to Bohemia,
its culture and language. That is, she is immersed, has gone

native, but has an escape hatch. The several women I've met who married Czechs and had Czech children they've chosen to raise wholly in a Czech context are the only individuals I've known who've gone native in an unmediated way, who seem utterly severed from American culture, the English language, a sense of home in America. One of them didn't even speak English to her children. These women didn't seem particularly happy, but did seem contented, or resigned, though that was only my quick read; they'd made family lives in Bohemia. They were home.

Human history, which is to say significant changes in the quality and nature of people's lives, has largely been a process of what anthropologists call cultural diffusion, and this process has primarily manifested, I submit, relative to the vagaries of reproduction. Rape and pillage, slavery, and arranged marriages between different tribes have been the main means by which groups have both genetically and culturally fused. The female slave, either the spoils of battle or simply a commodity between slave-trading groups, is brought into a foreign environment to labor and be sexually available; she is obliged to adapt unequivocally to the context of her commoditization. The female packed off to a foreign household in an arranged marriage is similarly obliged. But no one, chattel though she may be, arrives to such circumstances emptied, wiped clean of the circumstances into which she was born, chief among them her native language and the cultural values and assumptions it embodies. Every woman pressed into a foreign environment has been a kind of Trojan horse, and as such the primary means by which languages have evolved, cultures have blended, non-violent change has generally progressed. The greatest historical irony may indeed be that patriarchy, grounded in a sense of fixity and rigidity, of ownership and cultivation of land conceived as female, has always contained the fact of its own transmutation; which is to say that to the extent patriarchy is determined by oppression of women, the very means by which women are oppressed ensure the changes and ambiguities that undermine patriarchal determination.

No woman, of course, should be heartened by this. It simply means that throughout history women have been martyrs to the only positive change, the only social progress that has been possible in a world otherwise determined by frank brutality. Women have been going native since before we fell from trees, and this fact may be the primary reason we made the drop in the first place.

My father was in federal prison from early 1960 to early 1964, then again from late 1964 to mid-1967. He was then incarcerated with only intermittent stints on the outside for the following twenty-five years. That first seven-year stretch, my mother, four siblings, and I lived on welfare first in two different dilapidated houses in Elizabeth City, North Carolina, then in federal housing projects in Norfolk, Virginia. We lived on welfare, but did not "live" in those abodes in those cities; we waited.

There is a fundamental difference between living and waiting. One's relation to place is determined by this difference; I mean, a tourist or typical expatriate may be living in a quickened moment, but she or he is also waiting to move on; her identity centers on the ontological condition of waiting. When our lives center on waiting we are living in time rather than space; or, rather, we are living primarily in time, secondarily in space. To be "home" is to live primarily in space, secondarily in time.

A convict, as they say, does time; incarceration is less about confinement, space, than it is about time, a forced condition of intense waiting. Paradoxically, the convict's strict spatial confinement creates a condition of radical transit.

And the convict's family does time with him. In those dingy living spaces in North Carolina and Virginia we spoke daily, hourly, of when "daddy comes home." Our mother received daily letters, sometimes two or three envelopes in a single day, postmarked from the Harrisburg, Pennsylvania federal penitentiary, and then the Georgia federal pen. We were poor, but ate sufficiently well most of the time. We kids played, ranted, and laughed; we physically hurt one another and roamed luxuriously over the landscapes; we formed alliances with other kids; we dreamed mightily, but every aspect of life, waking and sleeping, was determined by a condition of waiting, of fundamental change to come. We waited for our father to get home from prison as some await a messiah or the end of days or, simply, death. We occupied our shelters as one occupies a bus station or a motel room. Indeed, before our father's incarceration, the only shelters we'd known, for the most part, had been automobiles and motel rooms. But on the road, the first seven years of my life, I'd felt a sense of home, in cars and motels, in the condition of transit. I was at home in movement through landscapes, felt most comfortably alive in a place, or in a particular relation to place, rather than in time. In fact, that period of my life seems timeless, the only phase when temporality was secondary to spatiality.

As a small-time con, a pathological liar, a soul-sick, profoundly deluded young man, my father created in all of his children this odd psychic condition of being only truly at home in transit, first by kiting checks and stealing cars all over the North American continent for seven years, and then by compelling us to do time with him for another seven. My mother was, literally, along for the ride. The one time my father tried to teach her to drive, in the desert, she nearly crashed into a cactus. For many years I assumed her a victim, but in recent years understood that her role was one of accomplice.

She chose that life, or rather, failed to choose another. She followed her man, then waited for him. Then she got sick and died. She did not choose her terrible death, but allowed a man to choose her terrible life.

The woman to whom I am tethered by the lives of three children grew up in a single apartment in Prague, as an adult has lived no more than ten minutes from that space, with the exception of those months she has spent in America. She visits cemeteries to place flowers on the graves of family. She is home. Her psyche is not determined by a condition of waiting, but by place. Her life is primarily spatial, secondarily temporal. I call her "Dom," which is close to the Czech word *doma*, "at home."

We will never overcome the structural dilemma that destroyed our marriage; now, divorced, there's no need to. We may intermittently grow angry, bitter. But I will never question the courage and decency of the mother of my children, her wisdom in knowing who she is and what she requires of life. I could never go native in Bohemia, but nor did I ever insist that she go native in America. I never attempted to chain her to my pathologies as my father chained my mother to his, though what bound them were manacles forged by my mother's own mind as much as by his.

Though our marriage is over, I will never stop being a faithful friend and parenting partner, and trust absolutely that Dominika will likewise never cease being decent and honest in her dealings with me. I'm hopeful that we will find further strategies for accommodating the separation from our children when they are *here* or *there*. But after some calm and thoughtful conversations, as well as a few arguments stuffed with rancor, we know where we stand with one another, in space and in time.

Adjacent Room

WHEN I WAS TEN, I HAD a lucid dream in which Jesus ate my face. He walked out of the bathroom of the motel room; everything was exactly as it had been when I fell asleep; my parents lay in one bed, my youngest brother between them; my sister and two other brothers slept in the parallel twin bed, and I lay on a fold-up cot perpendicular to the two. Jesus strode from the bathroom, white robed, smiling beatifically, and loomed over me, smiling. Then he lowered, but as his face approached mine, the smile changed to a grimace and his mouth opened and he growled as I awoke, screaming.

I was inconsolable, and unable to explain why I was sobbing, shaking. My mother was terrified by my behavior; my father, just weeks out of prison, pumped up from lifting weights and much meaner than when he was caught three years previously, was angry, threatened to beat me if I didn't calm down. I didn't know that swaggering, violent, muscular man who threatened me; he seemed nothing like the svelte, nervous, often funny young father I remembered. Just before we'd hit the road again, just a few weeks after he'd returned from prison to our hovel in Elizabeth City, North Carolina, he'd caught me working on a hole in the backyard; I'd started digging, with a battered shovel I'd found by the tracks, in the midst of the Cuban Missile Crisis a few weeks previously, and figured it would be a good idea to finish the project so the family would be safe if the missiles ever did start flying, but that man, that new, muscled-up, mean father halted my work, flailing me with his belt.

Obviously, I connected Jesus with my father, who, after his first prison term, often got religious when he drank. In Elizabeth City, I was carted off some Sundays to Baptist churches by great-aunts, and each summer attended Bible camps primarily because they fed us. I prayed, but always warily; it just didn't seem natural. My mother was a lapsed Catholic and spoke often of angels, but was otherwise sardonic on the subject of religion.

My oldest daughter Ema is scared of space aliens; sometimes, after watching something on TV—in the Czech Republic or the United States—that seems to take seriously the idea of flying saucers and extraterrestrials, she'll not be able to sleep. I'll try to comfort her, explain that they don't exist, that those phony documentaries are fun to watch but are not to be taken seriously. She says she understands, that she knows there are no such things as space aliens, but she just can't get the image of those big-headed, huge-eyed white creatures out of her mind. Nothing else, neither war news nor apocalyptic chatter, affects her similarly.

Religious faith comes in handy, and I fear I've denied my daughters the succor of believing in a higher power, a higher order, even though I myself believe in a power, an order. I just don't know how to name it, what to make of it. I'm not at all certain it's a valid source of comfort, except that assuming an order is to assume a purpose. I try to explain to Ema that meditating on the question mark at the heart of existence, the mystery of life, is important, that it's probably the most important thing a person can do, that all joy and awe, all art comes from such meditation. What I can't explain is how my love for her and her sisters wafts from my constant regard of that mystery; nor can I explain how that regard is at once utterly abstract yet wholly grounded in particulars, which is to say that she is the embodiment of my regard for the mystery of life and my unspeakable belief that life has purpose.

But such cosmic prattle will be cold comfort if I contract terminal cancer while my daughters are still young. How will I comfort them as I lie dying? Perhaps by dying calmly, but they'll want to hear something; they'll require words, stories. What if one of them should become terminally ill while still young? Yes, that is more to the point; how does an irreligious parent prepare a child to regard her own mortality?

Through the nineties, Western social scientists came to pluck and probe the Czech psyche with surveys and polls. Of course, Czech social scientists themselves exercised a new academic freedom to study attitudes so recently un-tethered from the Party line, and one conclusion of all that probing, by insiders and outsiders, was that the Czechs are among the least religious people on earth.

Spatially, Prague is defined by the elegant angles of spires, by the majesty of faithful places. Other European cities contain larger, busier gilt-encrusted cathedrals, but none more elegant in aggregate effect than the holy spaces of Prague.

All their lives, my girls have lived in the midst of Prague's splendor, and have regarded Prague's holy spaces as most Czechs do; that is, they regard cathedrals as museums, or simply as anachronisms. In America, churches and cathedrals are like working factories; they bustle; stuff gets done in them. In the Czech Republic, cathedrals are like castles, *just* like castles.

Ema watches the phony space-alien documentaries on Discovery Channel in Prague knowing that doing so will trouble her sleep. She is a reader, not a TV-head, but is drawn to that which deeply disturbs her.

Long before my father was caught and sent to prison, our mother told us there was an angel in the trunk, that it protected us, slipping from trunk to trunk, as our father exchanged one car for another, every fortnight or so, over our years of running, hiding from the FBI and innumerable local authorities. The angel was extremely pliable, and would slip out of the trunk and wrap around the car on snow-slicked mountain roads, would protect us from tornados. It never slept, and existed only to protect us in any car we occupied.

When I slept in the window, under my father's jacket or a scratchy army surplus blanket, I fixed on stars, when they were visible, and pressed my ear to the hard surface on which I lay. Did I believe there was an angel just below me? My father had not begun his drunken monologues about Jesus; I'd not attended a church service or even a single day of school. I thought I heard it whispering, once even singing. I recall being a little frightened of it, comforted but frightened. I did not wish to see it; indeed, I hoped mightily I would not glimpse it in action during a thumping torrent, wrapping around the bottom of the car, wrapping around the tires, as my mother said it operated, to make them sticky over the slick pavement. I couldn't imagine how it pulled off such a feat; I mean, I could not visualize the contortions, and simply didn't want to see it performing that particular operation, especially.

I didn't wonder if my family was the only one to have an angel in the trunk. I didn't wonder why God had blessed us with one, for I didn't even consider it an issue of deity. It was there on its own volition, out of a sense of duty I also did not wonder at.

I did, though, wonder why we lived that way, why the police wanted to catch our father and take him to jail, why he was so misunderstood. He could beat any man in a fight, any man in the world. Sometimes, under stars, in the desert, he'd drink Four Roses from the pint bottle, hold it in his lap and shoot at jackrabbits in the headlights as he steered. He'd rest his shooting hand on the door, dangling the pistol out the window, and steer with his knee while he swigged from the bottle. I can't recall if he ever actually hit an animal, though I recall the blasts ringing in my ears and static-laced mariachi music. We did not require our angel's protection in deserts; it was a wet-weather protector.

My daughters have grown up in the midst of Christian iconography, and they know the basic story of Christianity: Son of God, death by crucifixion, rising from death. I'm not sure what Ema, who is so sophisticated for her age, makes of the basic negotiation of Christianity, the suffering and dying for the sins of everyone; I'm not sure she thinks much at all about sin, though she does express strong concern for issues of justice. Are her space aliens sinful? Are they evil? I think not. They are just creepy. They have unimaginably advanced technologies, big white heads, and little white bodies. Their eyes are huge and liquid dark, their mouths tiny. They are said to take sleeping humans onto their spacecraft to conduct medical experiments, though everyone gets put back in bed. They make strange, quite lovely designs in wheat fields, though sometimes they also drain cattle of blood. On occasion they crash, and their damaged crafts and bodies are taken to a place called Roswell, in the New Mexico desert. They are more mysterious even than angels, for their purposes are more vague.

The Czech attitude toward death is the same as the Czech attitude toward all temporal authority; it's something to avoid and cheat. One avoids authority by lying low, playing along, maintaining a rich private life on weekends at the *chata*, the summer cottage. One cheats authority by stealing a little, just a little. The Czech motto before 1989 was something like, "He who doesn't steal from the workplace steals from his family." One avoids and cheats death in exactly the same manner; which is to say one lives focused on small particulars, tiny, manageable pleasures, and when the maw of doom creaks open, one simply recalls *Babička's* (Grandma's) *svíčková* (beef and dumplings with gravy), or the torrid beginning of a wicked affair, or both. To cheat death, in proper Czech fashion, is simply to ignore it.

And it's a profound ignorance chastened by a kind of shy mourning. In the Vyšehrad cemetery, just a few blocks from our home in Prague 4, many of the most famous Czechs are buried. Smetana, Neruda (after whom Pablo named himself), Dvořák, Mácha, Čapek, Němcová, are crowded among lesser lights that nonetheless sparkle for the Czech psyche. Among them, stashed in a crowded, untended row, is my daughters' great-grandfather, the father of their mother's father. He sparkles for no one, not even his descendents; his presence in such a prestigious space is more novelty than a source of familial pride. He'd been a minor "industrialist," therefore subsequently a tiny anathema to the Party. My ex-wife, Dominika, recalls him with wary humor as the crazy old man next door. He lived in the next-door apartment, with his ex-wife, Dominika's grandmother. They'd been divorced for as long as Dominika could remember, and through childhood she'd go next door to visit one of them, then say *"Ahoj,"* goodbye, saunter to the next room, and say *"Ahoj,"* hello, to the other. Divorced, the two occupied separate rooms of a two-room apartment, sharing the tiny kitchen and bathroom. The authorities had allowed them to divorce, but would not allocate another apartment to either of them, so they were forced to cohabit.

What bitter grace does such a circumstance engender? They lived on minuscule pensions, disliked one another, indeed on some level loathed one another. Dominika says they never spoke, lived crowded and juxtaposed though utterly apart. It seems they managed to live, truly, apart in separate rooms of a small flat, sharing vital facilities. I imagine a complex, silent understanding regarding kitchen and toilet usage, protocols so much more necessary and severe than those established by college roommates or young professionals similarly sharing living space and facilities.

And I imagine evenings the old people prepared for sleep, hearing the other shuffling behind the closed door, tuning a radio, snapping a light. I imagine an odd comfort, of knowing the other is there, dovetailed with loathing, a comfortable loathing unto sleep.

The divine is the ultimate other, and corollary to the question of its existence is the nature of one's regard for it. Should we "love" it simply because it exists? And if such regard is rewarded, and any other punished, should we not wonder at the efficacy of such coerced, or at least conditioned, feeling? Can it truly be love? And if it does not exist, what do we make of the love, which seems in every sense genuine, that some incredible individuals feel for it? What do we make of a true and faithful love whose object is nonexistent?

This is a well-traveled wood; theologians have answers, and I've considered a few, but am satisfied by none. I would be content to believe in the divine even if I am not able to love it. I would be content to know that it is in the next room, ignoring my presence as passionately as I try to ignore its little noises, the padding about, the clink of a spoon in a cup of tea. I would be satisfied with such a relationship to the divine.

And I would be happy if my daughter's projection of the mystery of life were not a space alien, but something domestic, something familiar, even a little odious if benign, not streaking across the sky, but sitting in a chair, reading, maybe, in an adjacent room.

The Big Easy and the Big Nasty[1]

As I write, it is late January, 2006; it's less than three weeks after my ten-day visit to what some are now calling the Big Nasty. On my first full day in New Orleans, a crystalline late morning, temperature in the mid-seventies, I took the Devastation Tour, by car, through Lakeview, New Orleans East, St. Bernard Parish, Chalmette, and, of course, the lower Ninth Ward. I'll discuss here Andrei Codrescu's *New Orleans, Mon Amour* in the context of my own complex feelings about the Big Easy I remember, and the Big Nasty it has become.

I'll wager that this collection of sweet and mischievous, sometimes artfully sloppy, sometimes tautly lyrical feuilletons had been in the works before Katrina, but got rushed into print by the publisher. The part of the introduction that speaks of the catastrophe, and the six Katrina pieces tacked on to the end, are the least persuasive, the least effective parts of the book. Codrescu's signature blend of irreverence and ironic self-righteousness is brilliant when he is acerbic, boring when he is maudlin. Luckily, he is almost always the former, and shades toward the latter only when he

---

1 Codrescu, Andrei. *New Orleans, Mon Amour.* Chapel Hill, NC: Algonquin Books of Chapel Hill, 2006. (978-1565125056, 273 pages, $14)

presumes to speak for a collective, for a "we," in this case, New Orleanians, and specifically New Orleanians who survived Katrina, and continue to suffer its consequences.

This gathering is gleaned from several collections of NPR and newspaper feuilletons, and it is very good to have these bits and pieces, this golden dross of an original and whirring mind, expressing such passionate regard for New Orleans. Andrei Codrescu is, I think, one of the most important poets in America, and much of his more resonant poetry is deployed in his ephemeral prose. There are a few longish essays (most notably "My City My Wilderness") in this collection, though even working long Codrescu must patch together more or less singular anecdotes. Everything Codrescu writes begins fast and ends neatly, often too fast and too neatly, though his beginnings tend to be more satisfying than his resolutions, which can't help but seem contrived in most instances, though when he is at his best his wrap-ups seem charmingly contrived, as is true of most Shakespearian sonnets, for example.

For all his appeal to an educated, liberal audience at whom he's ranted irreverent truth to power for more than two decades, his persona, I think, is fundamentally misunderstood. Codrescu's wacky, acidic critique of American popular culture issues from a sensibility steeped in Cold War sentiment; that is, one should never forget he is a Romanian Jew whose loathing of authoritarian structures is not abstract, but visceral, and whose worldview, on matters geopolitical, anyway, is very much right-of-center, pro-Israel, and Eastern/Central European. I bet that most of Codrescu's fans would be surprised to know that he did not jump on the anti-war bandwagon preceding the invasion of Iraq, and that his hatred of the Bush administration is grounded in a much more complex and nuanced critique than is generally true of the one articulated—to the extent that the left can be said to articulate any response to Bush these days—by the American left. Regarding the fact that he does not follow a liberal party line, Codrescu is always honest with his audience, but in a cagey way. He's a libertine, but he's not a liberal. He loathes authoritarian structures, but is not a pacifist, and, by extension, is not anti-military. He gets mileage out of goofing on commercial television, yet is probably the most media-savvy poet in America, and among the most shameless publicity hounds in that great pack of howling egos that is American poetry. Codrescu always sings his heart's truth, but does so, in fine Dickinsonian fashion, slant.

And that slant is one of the oddest, and for its oddness most valuable, angles from which American culture and society are being critiqued. Codrescu is first and foremost a poet, but one who reaches his audience primarily through prose and speech. He therefore reaches beyond the insular, coterie audience of American poetry, smuggling a kind of poetry into the ears of the most culturally sophisticated demographic in America, but one to whom poetry is on the same order as lacrosse and figure skating. He is a creature of late-night rants over emptying bottles and mounding ashtrays, a creature of ego-drenched fellowship among poets, individuals who assume themselves superior to the bourgeois masses, and unfettered by bourgeois conventions of morality. But unlike others of his tribe in America, Codrescu assumes the role of the poet to be the same as the role of the intellectual; he brings an Old World apotheosis of the intelligentsia to his role as American poet, a valuation that, with a populist twist, results often in lucid and original insight, a vision we can trust when Codrescu speaks for himself, but one of which we should be wary

when he presumes to speak for others. Codrescu is least persuasive when he presents himself as a New Orleanian, or when he
refers to "my" city:

> It's heartbreaking watching my beautiful city sink,
> but I'm at a safe distance ninety miles away and my
> heartbreak is nothing compared to the suffering of
> people still in the city. New Orleans will be rebuilt
> but it will never again be the city I know and love.
> —*From "Love Note to New Orleans"*

I remember four years ago discussing with my second wife
the prospect of leaving the city. A Czech who loves New
Orleans, she did not fancy relocating to Kalamazoo, Michigan.
Among the many immediate, concrete reasons I thought I
should take the job being offered to me at Western Michigan
University was what seemed then a rather silly one: I told her
that someday the Big One was going to hit New Orleans, and
described the doomsday scenario every New Orleans resident
lived with and joked about often; it was a contingency like
cancer, though more certain.

I was able to factor that contingency into my decision precisely
because I wasn't, am not, a "true" New Orleanian, and this is an
important aspect of my own efforts as a writer. For three decades,
I have been able to write only as an outsider, as a kind of resident
tourist. My thoroughly New Orleanian first wife, Betty, granted
me tacit permission to write anecdotal lyrics about her city, or to
write such poems from it. But that permission did not extend
insider's status, a condition of mind and spirit only very few who
did not grow up in the city may achieve. New Orleans, at least the
pre-Katrina New Orleans, did not often welcome outsiders into

the civic family, and I'm certain that this is as true for Codrescu as it is for me.

The Big Nasty will have no choice but to welcome outsiders and grant them insider status, but the Big Easy, defined as it was by a civic narcissism so profound it dazzled, did not require familial relations with anyone not steeped in its erotic dream of itself. Every New Orleanian, white and black, rich and poor, cultured and uncouth, stared into the mythos of the city and loved, unconditionally and unabashedly, what he or she saw reflected there. As Codrescu notes, "Later, when I started living there, I caught the Mythifying-of-New-Orleans virus, too." But this compulsion to mythify, as he puts it, is not a contagion of the body that any tourist may catch through casual contact with the locals; it's a condition of mind, of character, that can only occur by virtue of a lifetime exposure. I'll leave it to any true native to explain why this is so.

Now, New Orleanians stare into scattered shards. On the first day of my first visit to New Orleans after Katrina, from December 26 to January 4, 2006, I took that Devastation Tour with a friend whose uptown home had not been damaged. She had waited three months to make that tour, to see firsthand what was dead forever in New Orleans, her city, where she had been born and raised and has lived her entire life. I was honored to make that mournful circuit with her.

But I could not match her sadness, her soul-sickness. I'd never seen myself reflected in the city, had never loved my own image reflected in such a gorgeous, joyful, holy, yet corrupt and corrupting place. I saw miles and miles of redundant misery; I saw thousands of gutted, watermarked lives. But I didn't see anything of myself, or a dream of myself, and I think that Codrescu's claims of intimacy with New Orleans are dubious, or at best wishful thinking, a desire for a home that can never truly be home to anyone who came so late to it.

I submit that Codrescu, like myself, is a resident tourist; when he writes and speaks about or from the Big Easy or the Big Nasty, he does so with the authority of one of America's most distinctive and important voices, but also as someone who will never speak intimately. As a resident tourist, he has seen people loving themselves as New Orleanians, and as actors on the stage that is New Orleans. Whether white or black, straight or gay, male or female, privileged or destitute, Democrat or Republican, natives of the Big Easy were actors in a theater as large as a city, a theater in which they played a vast, egalitarian celebration of their lives. Before Katrina, Mardi Gras never ended in New Orleans; it simply started over. Carnival didn't end on Ash Wednesday. It began. Fat Tuesday was a culmination, but the cycle began again immediately. Nothing could change, really, or all changes were superficial, incidental. The rich remained rich, the poor, poor, the wretchedly poor, wretchedly poor. But all were joyful for all were seeing their idealized selves in the reflective mythos of New Orleans, a place that care did not forget so much as where it was postponed indefinitely, where the dead got danced into eternity and the rich and almost rich threw fake treasure to each other and to the poor, but where, too, the children of the poor were devoured, eaten alive by a social structure that was essentially racist, and that enlisted, diabolically and ingeniously, representatives of its victims as primary agents. The black power structure of the Big Easy was always in bed with the most conservative elements of the dominant, white power structure, and one pernicious result of this was a public school system so wretched as to be criminally so. The cycle of ignorance and poverty whirled within the grand cycle of endless carnival, the slow burn that began on Ash Wednesday and culminated in Fat Tuesday three hundred and some-odd days later, relative to the liturgical calendar, the endless theater of phony reciprocity, of falsely egalitarian joy.

As Codrescu knows, and expresses with subtlety and grace throughout his writings about New Orleans, the fact of the matter is that the Big Easy has always been a very sad city, a necropolis, visually defined more saliently by its garish cemeteries than by its architecture for the living, and in recent decades by statistics regarding young black men killing each other. It was, and now for different reasons is, a city inhospitable to children, former-Sheriff Foti's "Christmas in the Oaks" exhibitions—"Cajun Christmas" houses and the like produced exclusively by black prison labor—notwithstanding. And New Orleans was, as the Big Easy, as a primary tourist attraction, an urban area defined by a profound contradiction: it was a charmed space for debauchery, a space that was, as a mythical location, a celebration of Dionysian abandon, and yet, the seventies' gay renaissance notwithstanding, oddly prudish. Its legendary sensuality is largely, though certainly not exclusively, gastronomical and alcoholic; visual, tactile, auditory, and olfactory, but not primarily sexual.

Codrescu is at his acidic best lambasting power in all its social forms, and proceeds on the assumption that, as Hannah Arendt famously put it, evil is banality. In "Letter Home" and "Post-Duke Blues," he has fun beating an easy target, David Duke—who was, for the duration of his grotesque fifteen minutes, the pink piñata for anyone to the left of Rush Limbaugh—but more importantly he skewers David Duke's supporters, particularly those in that bastion of White Flight, Metairie, Louisiana:

> This is Andrei Codrescu, in hiding somewhere in Louisiana. It is the David Duke era. The Nazi flag is flying over the major car dealership in Metairie. A gigantic pelican, our state bird, with a swastika painted on his chest has been erected in the Metairie Mall. With their shades drawn, some Louisianians are bemoaning Duke's election to out-of-state newspapers.

This is just a rung above Dave Barry, but as ephemeral satire goes, that's pretty high. And the cumulative effect of Codrescu's commentary is certainly not wacky Dave Barry affirmation, but wacky Andrei Codrescu apocalypse. In "A Model for the World: A Louisiana Fairy Tale," citizens finally take notice of all the dire environmental news in their "Sportsman's Paradise," as its license plates tout Louisiana. "The people . . . stood in their beds, where rare forms of environmental cancer kept them, and wrote letters to their representatives." Why, even in the broadest satire, patients would stand on their beds to write letters is beside the point, especially given that even "fishermen momentarily dropped their nets overflowing with cadmium-full oysters and poisoned fish and took up the pen." Oysters in nets? Who cares? He's on a roll:

> Even people whose houses had long ago floated out into the gulf because of oil company-induced erosion grabbed their two-way radios and commenced to protest. Choking, gasping, puking, and reeling, the citizens of our state stood in the eerie light of toxic dumps and filled the gross air with appeals.

And the point of this cheerful hyperbole is to point out that under Governor "Buddy" Roemer, a Democrat who had postured as a environmentalist reformer, the legislature cut seventy percent of the budget for the Department for Environmental Quality, in effect neutering it. As Codrescu finishes his fairy tale, "things were back to normal. Nobody lived happily ever after. In fact, they didn't live at all."

This is Codrescu at his over-the-top, middle-finger best. He's most effective skewering power and its victims with the same rod: power for screwing us, us for letting ourselves get screwed. Doubly alienated, as a former citizen of a totalitarian regime and as an Eastern/Central European Jew, he desperately wants democracy to work, and is offended when it does not, for, especially as a European Jew, he is deeply aware of the slippery slope failed democracy becomes, that it indeed was, in the twentieth century, the greased chute to hell.

So many times over the ten days I was in New Orleans, I heard friends refer to "my city." "I can't believe what's happened to my city," an uptown friend, whose neighborhood had sustained little damage, sighed more than once. When I e-mailed my first wife to make a lunch date, I mentioned how stunned I was by what I'd seen on the tour the day before, and referred to New Orleans as the Big Nasty, adding that I didn't believe the most devastated areas would ever be restored.

She admonished me, with uncharacteristic self-righteousness, for calling her city—"my city"—the Big Nasty, and of course it was much too flip a term to use in an epistle to someone who had been that day intensely laboring to help friends gut their ruined home. The bond between survivors in New Orleans is powerful, and so is their aversion to outsiders, to those who simply can't understand what they have lost.

Whatever *they* have lost, besides their homes and a sense of unique civic identity, *we* have lost a play space that, at its best, was as pertinent an affirmation of sensuality to be the engine of the human spirit as has ever existed. We have lost a protean shrine to the dialectics of excess.

Most of all we have lost the American fount of a certain kind of irony, the kind that issues from an entire population taking fun seriously, a city that exists primarily to generate serious fun. In fact, in the Big Easy, serious fun was a religion, one that pinged off Catholicism, dovetailed with it, but which also managed to remain unmoved by papal frowns.

The humor I saw and heard in New Orleans those ten days was quite glorious, though laughter always petered out, was often punctuated by pregnant silences. The city that had been my home for so many years, in which I felt so comfortable even though I could never feel wholly a part of it, was in despair.

The Big Nasty is hope in the midst of despair. It's my beautiful first wife cobbling her life together, and my other friends on the cusp of deciding whether to stay and rebuild or leave and start over.

And it's also the singular talent and vision of Andrei Codrescu. I am moved and charmed by so many of his NPR feuilletons, such as "Whose Time Is It Anyway," "Indecent Exposure," "The Hidden Wealth," and "How Hot Is It: Summer Vacation in Louisiana." At his best in *New Orleans, Mon Amor,* Codrescu fixes a loving eye on New Orleanians; he exposes them—pre-Katrina— gazing at their own reflections. But it was their mirror, their city, not his, and certainly not mine, that they gazed into. One of America's essential poets, Andrei Codrescu is not at home in New Orleans, America, or Europe. He's rooted only in a point of view, in Codrescuville, let's call it, whose population is free, in every sense, and whose body politic, polymorphous perverse and a little drunk (more than a little randy), is dressed to kill and ready for some action; it is a place where history is an unspeakable burden and laughter is holy. Indeed, except for the fact that its sole citizen sees the obvious and reacts accordingly, it's very similar to New Orleans.

The Lear Years

I AM TOO OLD TO RAISE an infant daughter, but I do not regret, in any station of my psyche, her presence. She was a surprise, a jolt, a double take over the pink-tinged double stripes announcing her emergence from the void. She's a beauty, a keeper. She will be my Cordelia as I enter the Lear years, though I hope my two older daughters do not duplicate the proud king's other offspring. I hope to be doted on by all three, to whom I'll gladly give, in equal portions, all.

But, though I'm not certain if she'll "keep (me) young" as some say happens in such instances, I can testify that she doesn't make me *feel* young; I feel my fifty-one years more acutely when I hold her, coo into her face. I have never been quick with numbers, but one needn't be a math maven to know that as she's graduating from high school I'll be sixty-nine; I'll be seventy-three as she's moving the tassel on her college mortarboard and beaming as she traverses the stage. I'll indeed be in my Lear Years for most of her adolescence and young adulthood. Then I'll die, while she is still young.

I run; I lift weights. I'm quite strong. I'm a type 2 diabetic, but control the condition with diet and exercise. A lot of people on both sides of my family lived into their eighties, but they were mostly females; I don't know much about male mortality on either side, partly because there simply weren't that many males and, besides, I've lost contact with the extended families.

Dying's one thing, preparing quite another. It is strange to want to live less for yourself than for certain others, but that is the primary existential feature of parenting. When I catch myself being a little reckless, driving the freeway aggressively or walking a street most folks would consider dicey, or when the turbulence on a trans-Atlantic flight becomes extreme, what blazes through my mind is not an image of my doom but rather a tableau of my children in mourning, my daughters processing my loss.

I considered myself young for too long. I know I speak for many when I say that becoming not young, though it is a gradual process, can feel sudden in its effect.

A respected writer referred to me in a blurb on the back of my first book as "the best of the new poets." He was being too kind, indulging in the sort of inflated rhetoric that characterizes almost all blurbs, but I didn't stop considering myself a "new poet" for many years after. I don't mean I consciously thought of myself that way, but rather that it was an unconscious assumption into my forties that I was a "young" poet, a young man.

As a young man I worried about being a coward, which meant of course that I was a coward, and the coward's classic defense is to tempt fate, ostentatiously but in a calculated fashion. My teenage daughter will matter-of-factly announce, "Tata, I'm scared," after viewing something troubling on TV before going to bed. She is frank and unequivocal about the effect of *The Blair Witch Project* or a UFO documentary on her psyche. She is unashamed of her fear, and I envy her that, and am proud to have encouraged such a lack.

The main difference between my young self and my present one is that I am now at least a little comfortable with my cowardice, thought not as comfortable as my daughter is with her fear. Fear and cowardice are fundamentally different. Fear becomes cowardice only when lying about one's fear is a strong compulsion, when acting and speaking other than how one feels seems necessary. It's a guy thing. Machismo is the lie that transforms fear into cowardice, even, or especially, for the man who manages to act bravely.

As I age, my gendered identity becomes more ironic. I'm not afraid anymore of being laughed at. I'm not afraid of being thought a fool or a clawless monster. I'm not afraid of failure, not really. I'm not afraid of being neglected, ignored, at least in a professional sense. I'm not afraid of young men; I've met few I've calculated to be of much physical threat, but over the coming years I'll feel, of course, more and more physically vulnerable. As I age, my terror of extinction mellows, and I believe that this must be something chemical; surely the organism prepares for death. Perhaps as Eros mellows it also becomes a little fuzzy and attendant, like a pet, or a loyal fool who speaks in puzzles.

I love and admire those of my parents' generation, especially writers, especially poets, who have remained fierce, folks in their seventies and eighties who are still on the make in the fame game of the arts. They are the sort who, as they expire, will feel that they ran out of time, left things unfinished. One should hope that none—and I'm thinking of three or four who have been friends and mentors—feels bitterness; all will have completed significant works, won significant awards, fashioned legacies in the hearts of people like me who will be committed to keeping their good work alive as long as we are, and indeed passing it on with whatever portion of our own work warrants transmission, on the ether, via the hearts of the young. I hope to remain fierce, fiercely engaged, involved, unto dénouement.

But, more importantly, I hope to age in such a way that my daughters, and now especially the infant Ellie, perceive me as a fount of life, of vitality, of affirmation that there is never a good time to remove to the garden and retrench, that the good fight is always preferable to tending the garden.

Unless they are the garden, in which case I'll tend to them by being fierce, fiercely alive, involved, engaged, like Lear but without the royal hubris, I hope.

In New Orleans, in the mid-eighties, when I lived in the apartment between Bourbon and Dauphine that my landlady swore was the original House of the Rising Sun, a retired Filipino sailor, my neighbor, Bob, entered dementia quite suddenly. He was a wisp of a man, moving with unintentional stealth each morning and night by my backdoor, across the gangway overlooking the lush courtyard of our landlord and landlady. He occupied a "slave quarter" apartment, a single room and a bathroom that could not be accessed from the street. My apartment was three large rooms with fifteen-foot ceilings; my three floor-to-ceiling windows overlooked Rue St. Louis. Bob's only view was the courtyard, which I also had access to from my kitchen window and door. He and I shared a view of that bricked garden at the far end of which crouched a two-century-old voodoo shrine covered with charcoal "x"s, its crown lined with blue candle nubs. In season, the garden was resplendent with magnolias, and the odor from the gangway, the narrow balcony Bob and I shared, would be dizzying. Ferns, green fireballs, dripped from clay pots along the thirty-foot, mossy brick walls. Sometimes I'd lean on the dubious railing, newly whitewashed rotting wood, and smoke. I'd glance left and spy Bob staring down into the verdant decay, the funky little paradise of the courtyard.

No one ever visited; I'd have known. He lived on a pension from the US Navy; I discovered later that Judge Levy, the ninety-three-year-old owner of the House of the Rising Sun, whose forty-something wife, Darleen Jacobs, insisted that the building had, indeed, sheltered the storied brothel, rented to Bob for a pittance.

I responded to the first howls clutching a serrated kitchen knife; I could see Bob through his window naked under the kitchen table, the four kitchen chairs lined up on their sides as a kind of barrier. I scanned the room; no one else was there. The bathroom door was open. Empty.

I tapped on the window; his eyes caught mine and trepidation shaded to terror. I was holding a foot-long blade, saluting to peer through the sun-blazed glass. Even a sane person would have been frightened.

He would leave his hovel clothed and impeccably groomed each morning, and return in the evenings crazy, howling and chattering in three languages. One night he did not transition back to well-groomed sanity, but remained ensconced in madness in the morning.

On the third day of his howling, his screaming at demons and ex-wives, at an executive officer who had humiliated him, and an actual ghost, that is, something he called a ghost, I phoned the police for at least the fourth time since Bob had begun the slide; once again they were useless, insisting that they couldn't take him away if he wasn't hurting anyone or himself. I pointed out that he'd been barricaded in that room for three days; I'd seen him eating saltines, drinking water from the tap, but surely he would soon run out of food and then, by virtue of being unable to negotiate the trip to the store, would begin to starve. Wouldn't that indeed constitute his hurting himself? They told me to call when he began to starve, otherwise I should search out his family; only family could have him committed if he had a domicile, wasn't dangerous, and was able, even minimally, to sustain himself.

Bob didn't have a phone; all the mail for the three apartments in the House of the Rising Sun got shoved through the same slot; he never had any, not even junk. I peeked again through his window; he was huddled under his table, wearing only skivvies, scraping the edges of an all-but-empty peanut butter jar with a spoon. I looked for photos, family pictures; there were none. Only a faux oil landscape, a lake and trees, in a gaudy golden frame hung on the wall. There was a transistor radio on the fridge, a little TV at the foot of his bed. I considered entering and rummaging through his drawers for contact information, but didn't want to set him howling under such a circumstance. Technically, I'd be breaking and entering. I'd be committing a crime.

That night he wept, unceasingly. He didn't howl; he didn't admonish demons or wives, or argue with a ghost. He wept hugely through the night, moaning names, begging forgiveness. I couldn't sleep. I attempted repose on the couch, with the bedroom door shut, but his sobs seeped through the oak, and so I smoked and listened, and watched, from my darkened living room with the high ceilings and the high windows, from the midst of diaphanous shadows, the dregs of the French Quarter flow in and out of the Roundup, the cowboy/biker/transvestite bar on the other side of Rue St. Louis.

So this is what it comes to, I thought. These are the Lear years, the years of wretched solitude unto madness, of wandering in a storm of remembrance, of losing, losing everything.

That week, I was showing the BBC *King Lear* to my sophomores; I showed a Shakespeare play at that point in each semester, toward the end. It took four class periods, so it was a nice break from lecturing and Socratic class discussions. My students had a *King Lear* study guide I handed out each semester; they were answering questions, constructing little essays, frowning through secondary materials.

I'd taught other Shakespeare plays in that poetry and drama genre course for sophomores, *Hamlet* and *Richard II,* but had settled on *King Lear,* and taught it consecutive semesters. I was still young enough to identify with Hamlet, but Lear, I felt even then, spoke to my future. And as Bob the retired sailor sobbed at the end of his life, poured forth his boundless remorse, I realized that if his dementia had been inevitable, such loneliness should not have been. Where were his children? Where were the sons? The daughters? The issue of bad marriages, the issue of the ex-wives with whom he still argued, against whom he still raged in his demented heart?

Should I act as a son, take hold of his life, secure what succor might still be available in such a world? Should I play Edgar, the good son?

I spoke to Judge Levy, who was at least fifteen years older than Bob but incredibly lucid, in control of his every sense, and decent, deeply and quietly decent. The ancient fellow was married to a large, loud woman fifty years his junior, one of the most colorful and feared trial lawyers in New Orleans who could turn on the "Y'at" (from the Ninth Ward salutation, "Where y'at, Brother Man!") and woo any local, predominately black jury. Judge Levy, still on the bench (he would literally be forced to retire), was fully engaged in all of his business dealings, though Darleen ran the show. Judge Levy and Darleen Jacobs took control. They found out that Bob was indeed estranged from a scattered family, but that he had veterans' benefits that would cover his hospitalization, the extended care he would require. They were powerful people. I assumed they knew everyone, the mayor, the city councilmen, the police chief, everyone with power. Darleen Jacobs made a couple of phone calls and Bob was gone when I returned the next afternoon from the university.

In better days, Bob and I never spoke, but he'd watch from his window as I'd feed my birds, mostly mocking birds I'd raised through fledge into adulthood, when I'd set them free in batches of three to seven, in the same number and company as I'd received them from the Bird Rehab Center at the New Orleans Audubon Zoo. For several seasons, my first wife's friend, an anorexic uptown woman who did volunteer work at the Rehab Center, would give me batches of birds to rehabilitate, local babies who'd fallen from nests. I'd keep them in boxes, feed them by hand for weeks, clean their feathers, teach them to fly in the house, then set them free from the balcony overlooking the courtyard. Some got eaten by cats, but most would return to that balcony for many days following their release; sometimes four or five grown birds would arrive at precisely the same time early in the morning and beg to be fed, and I'd pad out onto the little balcony holding an open can of moist cat food and drop a pinch or two down each gullet before they'd flit away.

Bob watched, sipping coffee, and sometimes he'd dip his chin to me, not so much, it seemed, in admiration as recognition.

Stalin's Face

There is an urban legend in Prague that Stalin's marble face lolls at the bottom of the Vltava, the result of the huge statue on top of the cliff in Letná Park, high above the river, being literally blasted apart in the early sixties on Khrushchev's orders, or at least in the general spirit of Khrushchev's attempt to suppress memories of Stalin's brutal excesses. I thought of that face the other day when I was startled to see the face of my father, on the kitchen table, cut precisely from a photograph.

Of course Annie had come across one of the three or four photos Dominika keeps from twelve years ago, and cut out, meticulously with safety scissors, my father's head, but then abandoned it on the kitchen table, not intending to startle me, but simply because her interest in the project, cutting heads from photos and mounting them with glue onto cardboard, had waned.

Twelve years ago, he came back into my life after a hiatus of over a decade. I can't recall how he contacted me; he probably simply found my number and phoned. Since the day he left my brother and me at his sister's house in San Diego, in 1967, I'd seen him on three other occasions. In 1971 I was eighteen, and he insisted I visit him in Canada, a long cab ride from the Detroit airport; I'd paid for the ticket myself because he'd told me he'd reimburse me in cash when I arrived at his house across the border; he'd also give me enough cash to get through my first year of college. He paid for the cab, but, of course, stiffed me on the flight ticket and tuition. The second and third times were in 1975; he'd talked me into coming to see him in San Francisco. I did, and once again managed to lose money even as he enticed me again with promises of help with my college costs.

So, after my youngest brother, whom I'd not seen since he was seven, following but two weeks of renewed brotherly contact, talked me into co-signing for a pickup truck and immediately vanished in it; after I tracked my brother down three thousand miles away and took back the stolen vehicle, why did I allow my father to take over payments on that truck, thus tethering my meager fortunes to his? I knew he would use that vehicle as emotional leverage, as the means to keep me in contact with him. As soon as I stopped making the journey every fortnight or so from New Orleans to his woodsy abode outside of Tallahassee, Florida, a seven-hour trek, he'd simply, I knew with absolute metaphysical certainty, stop making the monthly payments on that vehicle. And so it happened. I've neither seen nor heard from him since.

He's only twenty-one years older than I. He was but sixty the last time I saw him, as his cutout head appears. He'd have turned seventy-three this past March; I've no idea if he is alive. He was deeply into Jesus when I was last in contact with him; he and his mousy wife, whom he'd wooed from prison through the mail, lived in a large trailer on several acres of land they actually owned. He'd helped her, for the several years after he got out of prison, with a business she owned. She was an RN, and he had gotten some sort of certification in prison as a "physician's assistant," whatever that is; together, they cruised the rural backwaters of Florida, Georgia, and Alabama giving checkups to simple country folks trying to buy insurance. Some of that cruising, before they settled into blissful semi-retirement, was in the truck my brother, his youngest son, tried, essentially, to steal from me.

That period, from 1990 to 1993, the first three years of Ema's life and three years before Annie would be born, were the nadir of my adult life thus far. Or, more precisely, they were the final years of my protracted adolescence, the years of transition from profound self-deception and self-involvement to ordinary self-deception and self-involvement. They were the years I was disentangling from my first marriage even as I was helping, as best I could, Dominika raise our daughter. They were the years Dominika and I began our shuttle between New Orleans and Prague, though my resources were wholly inadequate to such a jet-setting life. They were years of debilitating guilt and dogged effort to make my impossible life between two continents work, and to have a life as a writer and teacher. They were the years of expensive but merciful divorce from a dear and decent American, and marriage, with our three-year-old child in attendance, to a Czech at City Hall, on Old Town Square in Prague.

In the midst of this, my youngest brother, on whom I'd doted and whom I helped raise to the age of seven, found me and conned me, and my father, a professional con, reasserted himself into my life with the religious fervor of the utterly persuaded; every minute in his presence was filled with Jesus talk, and I loathed it, finally couldn't take it anymore, and stopped making the fourteen-hour roundtrip, those weeks and months I was not in Prague, between New Orleans and Tallahassee. The truck, with over a hundred thousand miles on it and more than five thousand dollars still owed, got repo'ed when my father stopped making the payments, and, of course, I got stuck with the bill, therefore pounded deeper into debt it would take me years to crawl out of.

My fury was dangerous. I wanted, literally, to kill him. I fantasized going to his trailer, walking through the screen door and, before he could grab the pistol he always kept close, against the law that forbids convicted felons from keeping such weapons, pounding him to death with my fists and anything close I could grab for the purpose of bludgeoning. I actually got in my car more than once intending to make the journey; I told myself I could control my rage, only smack him silly then leave, but if I'd ever gotten started hitting him I'd have been unable to stop until he was dead, and this knowledge turned me around once just outside of Mobile, before the long bridge past the battleship. I turned around because I saw Ema's little face in my mind and did not want to lose her, and knew that I would lose her, lose everything, if I beat my father to death.

My rage was, of course, cumulative. The truck, the five-thousand-dollar additional debt, were simply the final insult, the final sorrow. I was ashamed of my foolishness, how easily I'd been duped. I was ashamed of the fact that my motives for spending what little time I'd spent with him as an adult were tainted; I'd always expected, or wished, hoped to gain some sort of material advantage from contact with him. Deep down I thought he owed me for the twenty years he'd spent in prison, the six years of my childhood I spent waiting for him to get out of prison, the hope I wasted on being reunited with him. He owed me for punching my mother in the stomach to make her miscarry the child of another man she'd loved while my father was away the second time; he owed me for the times he beat me, once knocking me out with his fist. He owed me for the fact that I'll never be able to feel at home anywhere, that my childhood of running, always running from authorities—local cops, highway patrol, federal marshals,

FBI—made me incapable of bonding with any place, or at least I think that is the cause of my feeling at home only in transit.

He knew my motives were always impure, and that is why he conned me, ripped me off. He was punishing me for being like him. He was punishing himself, in a way. He wanted to make everything up to me, show me the One True Path, and what can be sweeter, more sweetly paternal than that? He wanted to give me Jesus, and as he prattled from a deep and faithful conviction, I literally yawned and checked my watch. He was afraid of death, but he was even more afraid of dying in total alienation from his children, especially his oldest son. He was giving me the opportunity to forgive him, to recall the sweetness rather than the horror, the times we all sang in the cars; the times he was tender and funny when I was very young; the thrilling times he shot at desert jackrabbits in the high beams at eighty miles an hour; the times we celebrated after he'd scored and we could eat as many burgers as we wanted; the times he sipped from a pint of Four Roses, all the car windows down, the smell of fresh hay and earth and whisky swirling around my head as the cool wind thrumped over all our bodies; the time, weeping, he squatted on his haunches to touch my face through the bars of a holding tank.

I should have forgiven him; I should have listened to him earnestly. I should have taken him in my arms and told him I was proud of how he'd been able to make a good life with a good woman against such staggering odds. I should have imagined what it had been like for him the first time he'd gone to prison, so young and so handsome; I should have imagined what older men had done to him. I should have imagined being gang raped, the physical pain and humiliation. I should have tried to figure out, doing genuine research, what had gone wrong for him, what had made him crazy, what had set him spinning across the American landscape with a beautiful, no less damaged young woman, accumulating children on the way to nowhere, to prison, to defilement, to bitter terror, to bottomless remorse, to a grown son he could not know, a son too self-absorbed, still too childishly self-absorbed to realize the opportunity he was squandering by hating his father with preternatural intensity, wholly unaware that that hatred was self-loathing.

Perhaps it's not an urban legend; perhaps Stalin's stone head does loll at the bottom of the Vltava, from whose muddy banks Rabbi Loew's Golem was fashioned. Neither Stalin nor the Golem were real; a man called Stalin, one of the earth's great butchers, walked the earth; he was a cagey, tenacious little paranoid, a vicious, ruthless paranoid responsible for the deaths of millions. But that is not what the mammoth statue represented; Stalin, the man of steel, the stern and loving father who led his people through more devastation than any population, other than European Jews and the entire continent of Africa, has ever suffered, towered in marble over Prague. The Golem, hulking protector of the Jewish ghetto, was as real as the desire for him, the need for his protection.

I'd like to think that Stalin's face lolls on the bottom of the Vltava, covered with mud, crusted and slimy with the mud of righteousness, the stuff of the Golem, his body, his essence. Not that I think Stalin should be forgiven; true monsters must be considered, measured, but not forgiven. Such a condition would represent rather a coming to justice, a mythical though wholly relevant justice.

My father never sought to hold power over others; not even his family, really. When he acted like a monster to his family, he always fell immediately into remorse. Whereas other men deserted their families to pursue lives of crime, he took us with him, included us, and, oddly, I think that was very decent of him. He always wanted to be decent, to be thought decent. He always wanted to be "legitimate" as he so often put it; he spoke often of making a big score, then starting a little business, going legitimate. Well, he did. He married a dear, stupid woman, was good to her, gentle, giving her all she required, and thereby purchased legitimacy. Surely over the past twelve years he's not returned to his old ways; surely he is too old. Surely he remains in the bosom of legitimacy, the bosom of Christ, or he is dead.

I won't seek him out; it's too late. My forgiveness has meaning only to my own heart, and is a necessary condition to my role as father. I'll keep his head in a little box in a drawer with the two or three other photographs I have of him. I'll remember that he could drive, literally, for days, stopping only for gas and provisions; I'll recall that he loved us enough to take us with him, and that he protected us the best he could, which was enough.

Poetry Is a Dead Art

"Though I sang in my chains like the sea."
—Dylan Thomas

IN RECENT YEARS I'VE BEEN HORRIFIED by the efforts of Poets Laureate of the United States to encourage more people to read verse for pleasure's sake. I've been equally horrified by a spate of books that would instruct us how to read poems and actually enjoy doing so. I mistrust anyone who enjoys reading poetry, as I do those who advocate for it. That love of poetry is a form of necrophilia.

Most good poems are about death; dying; fear of death; courage in the face of death; the death of love; the inexorable passing of time unto death; the death of passion; the death of civilizations; the death of the world; and they are about eternity, which is everything after death. Good poems can also be about love, but, as everyone intellectually and emotionally capable of appreciating (not to be confused with loving) a good poem knows, love is what we do most fervently and authentically in the shadow of our own mortality. Oh, yeah, and some poems are about the death of meaning.

I recall a Poets in the Schools gig in 1980; I was goosed out of Fayetteville, Arkansas, the big city in the area, down to Hope, Arkansas, before anyone who'd never screamed "Sou-eeee pig!"

had heard of Bill Clinton. Upon arrival, we stopped in a gas station for directions to the high school; we were greeted by a postcard rack, all of its dozens of slots filled with the same card touting that municipality as "The Watermelon Capital of the World!" Above the caption, a naked boy baby lolled in a giant, gutted watermelon.

I've puzzled over the iconography of that image for a quarter century. Of course, I at first found it hilarious, but, by the time we arrived at the high school, I was deeply troubled by the image of that infant, no more than three or four months old, steeped in watermelon sugar water.

What did the composer of that image think she or he was conveying? The watermelon did not appear neatly cut, but jaggedly split, smashed open with a blunt instrument or by being dropped. Did the infant belong to the composer of that image? Did she or he borrow the baby? And did the maker of that image take pains in the decision to place the baby in the melon naked?

What does a naked infant have to do with watermelons? I suppose I should mention that he was a white baby; if he had been a black baby, the image would have been odious and hideous, as well as troubling. Would the image have resonated any differently had the infant been female? I think not.

As I stood before a class of thirty juniors and seniors, reciting "Fern Hill" in a baritone almost as resonant as Thomas's but, of course, not as beautiful (and I wouldn't have dared attempt to affect a Welsh accent), I was suddenly overcome by the image of that baby boy ensconced in melon. Even as, through my inferior voice, Thomas was singing in his chains, I stared upon those kids, most a decade younger than I, and did not wonder what they were making of my shtick. Those were the sons and daughters of Hope, each baptized in watermelon sugar, each profoundly at ease in fields of melon. What could such lovely gibberish as I was spouting mean to them?

I explicated the poem deftly, in an audience-appropriate manner; I drew parallels to their lives, or at least to what I imagined their lives to be. I talked about innocence and experience, about Blake, about the Dionysian and Apollonian, about ecstasy and wonder, but they weren't buying it, for they knew, I could tell from their postures they knew, that the whole thing was about death, about a crazy Welshman drinking himself to death, about his not being able to get an erection, maybe, but definitely about his wanting to die, to be released from the lie of his life, the torment of his own egotism.

What could such a poem mean to those who had rocked in cradles of melon? I imagined all thirty of them in a patch unto themselves, swaddled in sweet juice, fated thus to be together on that particular day to hear a hippie prattle about a farm some guy goes a little nuts remembering, some guy who says he was happy when he was a kid running all over the farm, but that now he's chained up, but sings anyway, like the ocean. But the ocean's not chained up, so the last line of the poem doesn't make sense, especially to the children of Hope, the children of the Watermelon Capital of the World.

When the time came to get them to try their hands at writing poems, I told them to "free write" for ten minutes about the earliest childhood experiences they could recall, the earliest experiences they could recall having to do with watermelons.

There were bemused looks, wrinkled brows, a low rumble of discontent. I'd struck a nerve.

I told them that when I was a boy living in Elizabeth City, North Carolina, sometimes an aunt would bring over a watermelon, and that such occasions were glorious to my family. My father, I explained, had been in prison, and we five kids and our mother lived on welfare, so we depended heavily upon the kindness of strange aunts, our mother's mother's sisters, for fresh produce from their farms, and watermelons in summer were a rare treat, an occasion for celebration. I told them how we'd spread newspaper on the table, and our mother would carve the melon into many wedges, and we kids would sit half or fully naked around the battered aluminum table gorging on melon, not even bothering to spit out the seeds, and I could see that the children of Hope were a little mystified but also *with* me, in a way, that I was on familiar ground with them. I wanted desperately for one of them to break into rhapsody about being rocked to sleep in a gutted melon, but that was too much to wish for. I wanted one of them to shout, "When is a poem not about death?" so that I could answer, "Never," and perhaps there was a brilliant one among them who would then ask, "But what about joy?"

I am old enough to be the father of who I was then, and I have three young daughters, one of them almost the age of the children of Hope. Every time she sighs, every time she gazes over a book, every time she switches on the bathroom light and leaves her bedroom door slightly ajar so that the small glow will reach her, it is as though she is asking me, "But what about joy?"

No one who feels joy should want to write or read a poem about it, I would tell her, unless death is a wall, joy a lamp, and poems of joy the silly shadows we make with our hands.

Poetry is a dead art form; it has been dead since contagion magic became passé, sometime toward the end of the Stone Age. The only succor it offers is an assurance that others through the ages have been no less terrified than we, no less ridiculously, paradoxically hopeful in the midst of terror, but I suppose that's something.

Alan Levy 101: A Eulogy

Toward the end, he was marginalized at the *Prague Post*. One young colleague told stories of how he'd become little more than a copy editor and ephemeral columnist, knocking out a "Prague Profile" each week and otherwise vexing younger, sharper minds with dyspeptic egomania.

But none of them could touch him. He towered over the lot. He was fierce and talented; he had vision. On days when I allow my dress and demeanor to deteriorate because I've entered a half-crazed state of delightful work, Dominika, my Czech ex-wife, used to cluck and sigh that her husband was becoming Alan Levy, one of the worst dressed men on the planet. He earned this appellation traversing the city he loved above all others clutching a plastic bag in which he transported the stuff most people keep in briefcases, his terrible shirts spotted with *svíčková* or something less savory.

Rowboat to Prague, later re-titled *So Many Heroes*, was Alan's eyewitness account of the Soviet invasion, the only significant English-language record. It's a terrific book suffused with Alan's personality; like so much of what he published, it was less about its subject than it was about Alan Levy living that subject. Such writing is less journalism than meta-journalism, a journalist's self-regard against the backdrop of historical events and personages, and in the foreground of the professional ethos of "journalism." His other books included *The Wiesenthal Files,* an ambitious study of the great Nazi hunter whom Levy got to know during twenty years of Viennese "exile" from Prague; biographies of Elvis Presley and Sophia Loren; and monographs based on the last interviews ever given by Pound, Auden, and Nabokov. In addition, he published scores of articles in *Life, Look, The New York Times,* and the *Herald Tribune* among many others. Founding editor-in-chief of the English-language *Prague Post,* he coined the phrase, "Left Bank of the '90s," and so created the myth of Prague as a bastion of expatriate literary fervor. He was a deeply decent truth teller. To his credit, he was not a "nice guy"; he was loyal to the extent that loyalty served him. He was abrasively generous, always on the make, always self-promoting. He was unwavering in his assumption that greatness inhabited him, and so it did, at least in small measure, though perhaps in greater measure than any of us who knew him were willing to acknowledge.

He died of liver cancer in the spring of 2004; his last publications in the *Prague Post* damned the Czech medical system generally, and the hospital in which he was dying specifically.

His white hair was longish and unkempt; his eyes were ferret-like through black-framed, thick lenses. He had thick lips and big teeth. He was a noble-looking, ugly man. Levy possessed elementary to intermediate skill communicating in Czech; his German was much better, it seemed. His Queens accent made him even more repulsive to Czech ears than most non-native speakers. But he loved the Czech people and Czech culture, and I never quite understood from where such affection issued.

One of Levy's more interesting publications was an essay defending Ezra Pound. His argument was tortured but incredibly generous, even tender, toward the great poet and infamous anti-Semite. Levy had interviewed, in a manner of speaking, Pound in Venice toward the end of the Modernist giant's life. He managed to piece together a document that was subsequently published in a major venue and then turned into the centerpiece of a monograph, and in the entire "interview" Pound had spoken only a few gruff sentences over several days of contact. Levy's record of his time with Pound contained much description of the bard raising an eyebrow, looking away in disgust, smiling wryly, but for the most part refusing to speak. Interspersed throughout his soulful descriptions of Pound's pathological pantomime were Levy's conversations with Pound's wife, and Levy's musings about Pound's poetry and role as one of the progenitors of Modernism.

Written several years later, Levy's essay defending Pound against charges of anti-Semitism seems particularly odd given Alan's work on, his friendship with, Simon Wiesenthal. But Wiesenthal himself was controversial for having defended Austria's former president Kurt Waldheim against charges that as a Nazi officer he'd participated in acts of genocide. Levy, like Wiesenthal, insisted upon something like nuance, discernment, in our regard of evil.

Every July I tried to fold Alan's ego gently into the program for aspiring writers Dominika and I administer for an American university. On those occasions when I actually put him in the classroom, he taught, as one student put it, Alan Levy 101. I finally settled on having him give a couple of lectures, one based on *So Many Heroes*, one on *The Wiesenthal Files*. Of course, they were hits. But each spring preceding the program I had my ritual tiff with Alan. Always, the conflict was over money, but of course it was really about Alan's prestige, his sense of his own value.

He was and is entitled to the respect, even reverence that visionaries deserve but rarely are afforded. Alan saw in the Czech character an antidote to the poison of militant chauvinism, and he saw the paradox of the Czech heart, its penchant for joy in the midst of sorrow, as an evolutionary improvement in the human condition. In Prague, Alan Levy found a perfect place from which to peer into all that was American within him, a place where he could separate dross from gold.

And there was much more gold than any of us had the decency to acknowledge. His frank and unabashed pride in his work was a big, booming American pride, and it was uncluttered with envy and avarice; it was pure and fierce and full of happiness, full of love for the process by which people record their lives among the lives of others, inscribe the lives of others upon the scroll of their own lives.

In a little case by the door of the Globe Bookstore in Prague, on the third shelf down, there is something like a tribute to Alan Levy. A couple of his books, and a copy of the *Prague Post* from the day he died are propped there. One must squat a little to see this pathetic shrine, and though I'm glad there's something honoring Alan Levy in that English-language bookstore, each time I stoop to stare through the glass I want to kick through the insult of it, shatter its quaintness. A human being like Alan Levy does not deserve quaint tributes. He deserves tributes as fierce and purely motivated as he. He was a man of some greatness, if that quality is a fusion of vision and love of life, and of ability and will. Alan Levy managed to piss off enough Czech politicians, among them Václav Klaus himself, that he must have been doing something right as a journalist. He managed to record, in his Prague Profiles in the *Prague Post*, the large and small lives that composed the vast and complex interactions of Czechs with the foreigners, well meaning and not, who invaded their country after 1989. But Alan's legacy is both a sprawling and intricate one. A person must read his biographies of Sophia Loren and Elvis Presley against his interviews with Nabokov, Pound, and Auden, and one must consider his reams of interviews for the *Prague Post* against his eyewitness account of the Soviet invasion and his cold-eyed, unblinking study of the great Nazi hunter. One must consider his remarkable, paradoxical love for the Czechs relative to his being quintessentially, even obnoxiously American. Hearts and lives as large as his are rarely appreciated or adequately accommodated. The fact of the matter is that there would be little talk of Prague as a place of literary ferment if not for him. He was a saintly American huckster whose motives were pure, whose vision was true. To all who are not Czech yet dream of Prague; to all who would roam the world with a nugget of what is best about America lodged in their hearts, Alan Levy must not be forgotten.

Czech, Italian, Mexican Cuisine

MY DAUGHTERS HAVE GROWN UP IN the midst of writers, some famous, most not. Every summer of their lives they have witnessed their mother and me transform into the in-country coordinator and director, respectively, of a month-long writers program in Prague, which is to say a community of a hundred to a hundred and fifty, mostly American, aspiring and established literati. During each year leading up to start time, the Saturday preceding the first Monday of July, they've heard essentially the same conversations between their mother and me, the same amicable professional conflicts and conflict resolutions.

My ex-wife's and my professional relationship is eerily unchanged from when we were married. The fact that we are so efficient at compartmentalization is perhaps, ironically, one reason our marriage failed, but that's another matter. Suffice it to say that our failed marriage notwithstanding, our partnership, parental and professional, at least so far, thrives.

And the professional aspect of our partnership centers on annually mounting and executing (of course with the assistance of talented colleagues) an academic program that is entering its fifteenth year, and that resonates significantly in the far-flung, academic/cottage industry of creative writing.

On Sinkulova in Prague 4, near Vyšehrad, the park on a hill overlooking the Vltava where the most ancient vestiges of Prague culture are commemorated, stands the five-story apartment building my ex-wife owns with her lawyer brother. Since the divorce, when the girls and I are in Prague I reside in an apartment on the *prizami*, the ground floor, and the three girls shuttle between my space and their mother's on the fourth floor. The two older girls are not happy about the divorce (our toddler Ellie, alas, is oblivious), but are adjusting well in no small part because their mother and I have managed our rancor quite deftly.

And, indeed, the Prague Summer Program, our mutual investment that lies vaulted so much deeper than monetary necessity, an investment not unlike parenting, mitigates our rancor. Dominika's ego investment in the program has virtually nothing to do with art and pedagogy. Brilliant and insightful but void of artistic ambition, she relishes managing the infrastructure of the program, making the proverbial trains run on time, which she does exceedingly well. My own ego investment is more complex, precisely because of my artistic ambition.

On Sinkulova, just two doors down from my ex-wife's building, is the Worst Restaurant in the Free World, as that world has expanded to include Central Europe since 1989. If there is a worse restaurant, in Warsaw or Cleveland, Bratislava or Iowa City, it would be worthwhile to dine there simply for the uniquely negative experience, rather in the spirit of attending an elementary-school musical performance: One's tenderness toward existence may be deepened by an affection for the performers, their humanity, that is very much in spite of the quality of their performance.

Over the past five or six years, despite its proximity, the girls and I have dined in that establishment but seven times, and each instance of patronage we swear will be our last. Of course it's become a running joke. "Why don't we eat at that Italian place?" There are several good Italian restaurants within walking distance, but the question thus simply posed points two doors down, and the resounding response is always a unified negative. And yet from time to time I want to give the place another chance, and that, of course, has become part of the joke. I threaten to take the girls there, and they talk me out of it. I even plead a little, insist that we should not give up on the place, that the previous disasters there could have been coincidental, as statistically unlikely as seven such disasters in a row, over five or six years, may be.

I believe in creative writing, the pedagogy, and am proud of the work that gets done in the Prague Summer Program over its four-week duration each July. Yes, there is much silliness, intellectual dishonesty in the academic business of creative writing, but no more so than in the humanities generally, and certainly no more than in the social sciences. The silliness has to do with encouraging people who don't read to write, and that, of course, is the fount of its intellectual dishonesty as well, because at its best creative writing has everything to do with passionate reading. All the same the radically egalitarian assumption from which the teaching of creative writing has proceeded over the past forty years, that any Johnny or Sally can make authentic poems and stories, an idea as naïve, perhaps, as it is finally profound, is among the more world-transforming blossoms of the past century—as useful to the planet as the peanut, I contend. Some giants of world literature may condescend to our little academic business, the cash cow of most English departments in America; they may smile down indulgently upon those of us laboring in the creative writing mills, but finally even the most haughty Nobel short-lister must grudgingly admit that all serious literature benefits immeasurably from the complex network, the veritable four-generation legion of readers/writers that the academic/cottage industry of creative writing has produced.

The Worst Restaurant in the Free World is clean, the service efficient. It has a nice little bar, and when my ex-wife wants draft beer, I sometimes carry her porcelain pitcher that holds exactly two beers the forty meters or so to the Worst Restaurant in the Free World, where the laconic waiter/busboy/bartender carefully fills it such that I pay for, and my ex-wife therefore is compelled to slurp as she cooks for the girls, very little foam.

Dominika does not hate writers, but she brings to their care a polite disdain. She judges us a little ridiculous, as she years ago likewise judged her father, a middling crime novelist who had mild success for all the wrong reasons during the period, after the 1968 Soviet invasion, called Normalization.

I'll not here recount all seven of our previous forays into the Worst Restaurant in the Free World; suffice it to say that each time one or both of my older daughters accompanied me, and each time the service was fine and the food wretched. It is difficult to say the common fault from which all the meals suffered, except that whoever has occupied that kitchen seems not so much indifferent to quality as bent upon defiling all standards of culinary decency. When I was still consuming mammal flesh, I ordered a pork loin that arrived nearly raw, and when I requested that it be cooked through the waiter was incredulous, it seemed, not so much at my request as at the likelihood of the kitchen granting it. On another occasion, a chicken breast appeared likewise half raw.

Once, Ema, my oldest, ordered a pizza and what arrived at our table was clearly from a box. When she requested more tomato sauce in perfect Czech, the thawed pie was swept away and returned in ninety seconds with raw tomato slices scattered over it.

So when the Worst Restaurant in the Free World changed its sign to claim "Czech, Italian, Mexican Cuisine," the girls and I had a hearty laugh. Passing the place two or three times a day, we goof on the sign, its triadic claim of anything remotely resembling an authentic "cuisine." Our running joke has been that I'll give the place just one more chance, and of course I've been genuinely curious as to how and in what particulars that wily cook may render tortillas, beans, sour cream, and cheese inedible.

Dominika's patience with diva writers has worn down over the years to a few frayed threads. She is generally patient and classy, but I fear that this year or next she will snap and throttle a famous American poet or novelist. Some famous writers, like folks generally, are low maintenance, and some are high. My ex-wife regards it as my divine duty to her, my primary colleague, to vet properly and subsequently hire only low-maintenance faculty. I have gotten much more astute over the years at vetting writers in this regard, but sometimes a High Maintenance slips my guard, or a Low Maintenance morphs with freakish suddenness into a High.

I've tried to explain to my ex-wife that sometimes HM's are worth the massive pains in our collective ass they cause, that a smashing performance in the Ypsilon Theater Reading Series is worth a 3 a.m. cab ride to the Centrum to unlock an apartment with the very key that the HM has jiggled in the lock for an hour and a half. Indeed, when a Pulitzer Prize or National Book Award spends quality time with students and also gives a smashing reading, well, that's worth moving an HM from an elegant apartment into the Hilton, on the program's nickel, at 11 p.m., because there is entirely too much street noise on that verdant and quite lovely urban meadow island of Prague called Kampa. But Dominika is unmoved by all implicit and explicit claims of status among American writers. She simply requires that everyone behave with an appropriate measure of humility in her country, and that they not be massively stupid, which is how she regards anyone who can't work a key into a lock, or sleep with a pillow over her head for a single night.

Last week Annie was famished after school, but we were running late for an afternoon appointment so didn't have time to hoof it to any of our favorite eateries in the neighborhood. I told her I really, really wanted a burrito. She cracked up, finally relented, though she predicted with canny prescience that we would regret the meal.

It was large, filled the plate. Inside the flour tortilla, which was brittle as a cracker, was an ugly blend of canned black beans, canned corn, cubed chunks of chicken, clumps of unmelted white cheese, all held together by a sickeningly sweet, heavy barbecue sauce that had no doubt arrived on the Delvita Supermarket shelf in a plastic container. A type 2 diabetic, I simply couldn't eat much of it after the first taste, but I picked at it, and Annie picked at hers. She gave me wry, I-told-you-so glances, and I promised I'd make her something good for dinner. The beer of course was fine, and she ordered a second Coke. I smiled at the waiter when he removed our plates, and told him the food was "*strašný*," terrible. Then I tipped his sad silence hugely.

The Worst Restaurant in the Free World is in a very nice location. It seems to do a steady business, but mostly from the bar, not the kitchen. What moved the owner to transform a criminally bad Italian restaurant, that is, one advertising itself as Italian and grotesquely approximating such cuisine, into one still worse that offers Czech, Italian, and Mexican food, all execrable? It would be so easy to construct a mediocre burrito. All the necessary ingredients may be found in Prague, even a proper piquant sauce, even refried beans.

At first I was going to have Ema translate the following into Czech, but then, given that the restaurant's menu is in English as well as Czech, I simply slipped the following in an envelope under the door after hours:

Dear Owner,

Because for three or four months each year I live only two buildings away from you on Sinkulova, I have dined several times in your establishment, hoping after my first visit that your cook would be fired or die of natural causes, and each time after that first visit I have been as deeply disappointed as I'd been on that first visit to your establishment, and yet your food is so aggressively bad I'm intrigued. It is difficult to believe that food can be so bad unless the individual preparing it actually desires that it be awful, and so I can't help but wonder as to the motivation of your cook, who, though he or she should be in prison, has evidently found job security instead among the free citizens of the Czech Republic.

I am an American who spent many years in southern California eating good Mexican food, and will gladly teach your cook how to make a burrito. First of all, you need to steam your tortillas. Second, you MUST purchase or prepare refried beans. Third, nothing you put in the burrito should come from a can. Fourth, you must find genuine salsa; I've seen it in stores in Prague, so I know that with a little effort you could acquire it. You could also make it yourself with fresh ingredients, chief among them tomatoes, peppers, and cilantro.

Please, friend, burn your menus and start over. Do not advertise "Czech, Italian, and Mexican Cuisine." That is very, very stupid. Regarding at least two of those you and your cook (I pray that you are not the cook!) obviously know absolutely nothing. Have your cook learn to prepare seven or eight dishes very well. Consult cookbooks; consult the Internet. Consult your mothers. There are easy ways to learn to prepare good food. You are so conveniently located that if you served any decent food at all my daughters and I would dine with you at least once a week. If you served several good dishes you'd certainly make more money. Don't you want to make more money? It would take so little additional effort.

If you would at least like me to teach your cook how to make a decent burrito, please feel free to contact me at . . .

I've not heard from the owner, and Ema has raised the intriguing possibility that the Czech, Italian, Mexican restaurant is a money-laundering operation. Perhaps so. Be that as it may, I feel better for having made a neighborly gesture, for having at least attempted to improve the quality of life on my block.

Such civic mindedness is of course diluted by the fact that I am not particularly enamored of Czech culture. Oh, I like English translations of twenty or so Czech novels, most of them by

Kundera, Škvorecký, Klíma, Hrabal, and my old friend Arnošt Lustig. I like Dvořák's music. I like Havel, though not his plays particularly. But I could never bring myself to do the hard work of learning Czech beyond a survival-skill level. What I can understand does not compel me deeper. The simple fact of the matter is that I did not love my Czech wife enough to learn to love her in Czech, and my older girls required me to be a fount of English through their formative years, as even the toddler, who speaks to me in Czech, already requires me to gush forth English in reply. To condescend from ignorance is the essence of folly, but the best I can say of Czech culture, from the depths of my ignorance, is that it is quaint, as quaint as an awful Czech, Italian, Mexican restaurant.

In the nineteenth century, cleaving to Czech identity made sense. It no longer does, anymore than Texan or Californian identities make sense beyond the most superficial and atrociously nostalgic boundaries of regional identification. To the extent that Czechs and other small populations of European ethnicities can become, over the next two generations, European, Czech culture, as such, is already enveloped in mist. Ask Milan Kundera, a world-class Czech writer, why he lives in Paris and composes now exclusively in French.

Europe must duplicate the American experience internally. That is, ethnic groups must lose themselves in a common European culture, a common European society. Czechs must become, in their hearts, immigrants in a new Europe. But what will be the common language? How will Europeans communicate across ethnic chasms? Listen to the radio in any European car. Watch television in any European home. Listen to the chatter at the bar in any big-city European dance club.

And like immigrants they must husband a nostalgia for what

they were, or, rather, what they dreamed of being, but in full knowledge that they may never crawl back into the wombs of their Czech mothers, certainly not into the womb of ancient Libuše, who, legend has it, stared down from Vyšehrad to the Vltava and received the vision of a great city. I submit that what she saw was not a Czech, but a European city.

As an ingénue, Dominika wanted desperately to escape Czechoslovakia, all the better if doing so entailed marrying an American; as a tough and beautiful middle-aged woman, she has embraced all things Czech. She and her lover, a sweet, deeply good Moravian named Igor, go off on weekends to hike through the countryside, hunting mushrooms. They ride the cultural slipstream of anti-Americanism in the twilight of W's disastrous reign, and I do not blame them. In spring and summer into fall, the Czech countryside is a good place to relax, and if there is one defining feature of Czech culture it is that Czechs relax with a vengeance. Relaxing is how the Czechs outlasted each of their historical oppressors. My Czech ex-wife is not good at relaxing, but she is brilliant at organizing and managing the relaxation of others. In this, she is very German, like most of her ancestors.

In the summer, as is true of the residents of all European cities, Praguers spend much more time out of town than in, lounging in their *chatas*, their little summer cabins, tending lazily to gardens. Precisely when we desire the best and brightest, the mighty blossoms of Czech culture to participate in the Prague Summer Program Lecture Series and Ypsilon Theater Reading Series, no one is available; everyone is sitting shirtless on rustic porches, gazing into woods, with the supreme and fortunate exceptions of Ivan Klíma and Pavel Šrut, two of the best writers still residing in the country.

I believe that the Prague Summer Program is a good thing, but when I explain why it is good I become a salesman. I am quite a good salesman, but I hate what happens to language when it is pressed into the service of selling. Persuading someone that a July spent in Prague reading and writing should not be the same as persuading her or him to purchase a particular brand of mayonnaise, and yet the language presses both cases similarly—as if flogging a product. Suffice it to say that the Prague Summer Program is a very good product. Participating in the program, many bright though provincial Americans are dazzled by the city, and that somehow transmutes into a more inspired focus on the products of their big American literary ambitions. They learn to expand and craft, or better craft, their creative efforts, and simultaneously learn the outline of Czech literary history. The dovetailing of creative writing and culture studies is a unique feature of the program. Predictably, over the program's duration, a lot of late-night drinking and libidinal cavorting occur among the rank and file, but most buck up in the classroom. I am proud of the quality of the work my colleagues and I have done in the Prague Summer Program.

I sometimes hate the Prague Summer Program and all established and aspiring writers, but only for a few minutes at a time. More often I am embarrassed for my fellow writers, no matter where in the pecking order they fancy themselves to be. I am particularly embarrassed for and by many poets, who, when they mount stages, transform into the most incredibly narcissistic assholes. It is something about lyric poetry, something about the range of personality types that latch early onto that mode of expression, which renders otherwise decent, sensitive, intelligent people into closed systems of self-congratulation for the duration of a performance. Alas, this is particularly true of the very young and clueless, early-twenty-somethings who come to Prague to drink, screw, and be affirmed. On Friday nights when the students perform, fledgling poets will sashay one after the other in five-minute intervals, onto the Ypsilon stage and chant unabashedly the most linguistically unsophisticated, intellectually vapid, aurally awkward, puerile, sometimes even scatological nonsense imaginable. Of course my job is to lead my faculty in their somber task of purging young poets and writers of such stuff, but in a world in which students are customers the operation must be performed so deftly that the student so corrected feels she or he has also been affirmed.

I am proud that my daughters are good, strong critics. They have noses for fulsome praise and can efficiently process thoughtful, strong criticism. Ema is becoming, alas, a very good writer of expository prose, and Annie will someday, I predict, compose airtight legal briefs. Both have sat through many literary readings, and have offered, to me in private, spot-on critiques of famous writers' performances more scathing than anything one sees in the top-tier literary journals these days. Like their mother, though for different reasons, they're indifferent to writers' claims of status.

I don't know how many more years my ex-wife and I will be able to run the Prague Summer Program. I dream of quitting it, of quitting the last formal alliance with my ex-wife other than the one our children necessitate. I would love to have, like other academics, three unencumbered summer months each year to dedicate to my own work. But when I imagine quitting, working up the nerve to quite, I feel panic. My life rhythm with the mother of my children, our failed marriage notwithstanding, is simply too comforting, too important a part of our children's lives, and I do not want to deny our youngest, conceived in the midst of our untethering, the program, the spectacle of her parents' transformation each July into a man and a woman with a common purpose other than her and her sisters' well-being, though, at bottom, regarding all things, including the program, that is our common purpose.

The Animals We Must Become

SHE WAS THREE AND A HALF. Her mother recently had placed her *doondie*, her pacifier, on the fourth-story window ledge of our apartment, in Prague 5, for the pigeons to carry away; she and her mother had negotiated such an end to her sucking habit. I'd been reading to her for more than a year. She was wholly accustomed to that intimacy. I'd read to her the *Lion King* picture book, and she'd suddenly leap to the dresser at the foot of the bed and strike a lion pose—on hands and knees, chin lifted—and roar.

It was her idea that I tell, rather than read, her a story. She certainly didn't want me to stop reading to her. She simply wanted a telling in addition to the reading.

The distinction is interesting, and I'm now a little amazed that she, at that age, made it. But I had indeed from time to time told her the classics, "Three Little Pigs," "Hansel and Gretel," "Cinderella," though in the latter two cases she was familiar with the plots from their Czech versions. No, she wanted me to make up something. She wanted something that would be all hers.

She was three and a half and pressing me for original narratives. And she wanted the stories to be about a horse. She insisted. A flying horse.

Because I lack imagination, I glommed onto the only flying horse of which I am aware, and the Pegasus stories were born.

For seven intense years, and two more intermittently, telling Pegasus stories was one of my chief duties on this planet. I concocted at least one a day, often two, sometimes three or more, and each ran at least five minutes, sometimes as long as fifteen. Only the cosmos knows how many words I thus poured into my baby's world, but that those stories, literally thousands of them, affected her deeply, there is no doubting. By her bed, now, upstairs in her room in her mother's apartment in Prague 4, the last time I looked, were *Ulysses, The Interpretation of Dreams, Hard Times, The Elements of Style,* and *Wuthering Heights,* in addition to Czech books by Bohumil Hrabal and Pavel Šrut. At eighteen, she has acquired my habit of reading several diverse books at a time. But if I tell her one night that a new Pegasus story has flown suddenly into my head, she will be delighted to sit still and listen. Indeed, extricating myself from telling Pegasus stories was extremely difficult, and for a number of years, even after I'd begun telling Annie Big Bear stories (six years younger, she would, as early as four years old, listen cagily to her sister's Pegasus stories, but soon insisted upon her own creature and magical circumstances), Ema required that I continue telling Pegasus stories right up to the border of puberty, and a little beyond. Double duty was exhausting, especially given that transitioning from composing for a discerning pre-adolescent, who was already reading Harry Potter books, to a five-year-old much less cerebral by nature than her older sister, often produced within me a kind of psychic vertigo.

Every story-telling parent knows the drill. You have to come up with a formula, and a good half-minute is given over to that formulaic entrance to the story.

> *Once upon a time, a long time ago, there was the sweetest, bravest, smartest little girl in the world named Ema Katrovas.*

A father can only hope that his daughter, hearing herself referred to this way thousands of time through childhood, will better weather bouts of adolescent self-loathing than otherwise.

> *One day, she said to her tata, "I feel the tickle!"* As I tickled her on the back of her neck. *"You know what that means!"*
>
> *"Yes, Ema,"* her tata answered, *"but it's much too late for an adventure in the Magic Islands!"*
>
> *"No, Tata,"* Ema corrected, *"You know that whenever I feel the tickle I must do my duty!"*
>
> *"Okay, Ema, of course you're right."* Ema's father was always reluctant because he feared for her safety, but he also knew that she had what amounted to a sacred duty to the Magic Islands' creatures and more or less human inhabitants.
>
> *And Ema jumped out of bed, ran to the window, opened it, and yelled, "Pegasus! Pegasus! Pegasus!" And POP! There he was! And she jumped up on the windowsill, onto his back, and he took off like a rocket!*
>
> At this point, a lot of hand jive: *He flew above the clouds then swooped up up up then dove down then back*

*up then straight as a ray of light, and Ema hung onto his
silky mane as he dove straight back down, through the
clouds and the Magic Islands lay before them.*

There were thousands of Magic Islands, a sprawling archi-
pelago, and there were a few islands to which she'd return again
and again because she became attached to the creatures and/or
"villagers" there, but she is certain, even now, that there are still
many, many unvisited islands.

She would only feel the tickle when there was a problem that
only she could solve. Sometimes the problem was self-evident, a
sleeping monster or a mean and nasty awakened one; a nefarious
wizard who could pop up anytime on any island and was my last
resort when I was just tired or distracted. Of course Pegasus carried
accoutrements in a leather pouch draped over his neck, chief among
them a magic rope (my apologies to Wonder Woman). But Ema
solved the villagers' problems usually by negotiation and sly,
though benign, trickery.

I actually tried to transfer Pegasus, David Beckham-like, from
Ema (Manchester United) to Annie (Real Madrid), but neither
would hear of it. So Big Bear was born.

*Once upon a time, a long time ago, there was the
sweetest, smartest, most mischievous little girl in the
world named Annie Katrovas. And one day she said to
her tata, "I feel the tickle!"* I tickle her forehead. Ema's
SOSs were felt on the back of her neck, and Annie's
on her forehead.

"But Annie, it's much too late for an adventure!" Her
father, she already knew from eavesdropping on her
sister's stories, was something of a wuss.

> *Annie just laughed, kissed her tata's cheek* (which Annie would then do), *jumped up and ran to the closet, opened the door, and shouted, "Big Bear! Big Bear! Big Bear!" Then jumped into the closet, and she was rolling on the grass in front of the Old Oak Tree and there was Big Bear!*

In the beginning, the first two or three years, Big Bear carried her on his shoulders to Pixie Village, right across the road from the Fairy Grotto, Annie's favorite destination, but, though he was a fast runner, she required swifter transport, so a flying broom, named Amelia, was commissioned. In the beginning, her nemeses were a gremlin for whom the worst punishment was a forced scrubbing in the nearest pond, stream, or lake, and a Bad Witch, whose sister, the Good Witch, was rather like the old fellow who created and demonstrated 007's gadgets. The gremlin faded away and the Bad Witch, alas, was rehabilitated, though sometimes I consider bringing them back in their original forms because (story-telling) life without them is more challenging. Annie is eleven and hounds me for Big Bear stories; I fear I am almost storied out, because I always put her off as long as I can. But both girls are excited as to what magical creature and circumstance awaits the baby, three-and-a-half-year-old Ellie.

The three of us now form a committee on the subject. As chair of the committee, I've swatted down squirrels and lions, out of respect for Rocky and Bullwinkle and C. S. Lewis. I'm leaning toward a monkey who will transport Ellie to a jungle, but I haven't figured out how he's going to get her there, given that wings are *verboten*. I'll probably have her jump into the closet, like Annie, and just have the monkey waiting for her *à la* Big Bear. She'll roll out from the mouth of a cave, probably, and he'll be there, ready for adventure.

All writer parents with whom I've ever discussed the matter of storytelling and its relation to parenting, as well as to the writer's life, have spoken, some even solemnly, about those worlds they created for their kids as though the magic creatures they fabricated and deployed across those fantastic landscapes were intimates. And of course they are. Those animals are our totemic selves, the animals we must become in order to be most strangely other, yet comfortingly familiar to our children. As an all-white flying horse I was charged with transporting Ema, as I'd carried her on my shoulders well into elementary school, and because I, being an American, was the reason she didn't live just in Prague but traversed an ocean through the air once or twice a year all her life. Annie by contrast requires me to be earthbound, large, dark, and furry, very much as I actually am.

The animal I am to each of my daughters is an enabler, a protector, but one that does a girl's bidding, assists her in important work. Pegasus was laconic, but often eloquent, if I do say so. He sounded a little like Mr. Ed, and I simply couldn't keep such a voice going for soliloquies, so he usually spoke only when spoken to, and then only, like a good soldier, precisely the information requested. For a while, a couple of years, actually, there was a flying colt, Little Pegasus, who lived on one of the Magic Islands, and sometimes he'd show up with Pegasus and Annie would ride on him, but the two of them, Ema and Annie, even when Annie was four and five, were simply too contentious to occupy the same narrative more than occasionally, and Annie always pushes plot points that I must integrate into any narrative she occupies, and those points are usually contrary to the style of narrative in which Ema feels most comfortable.

On a few occasions the girls talked me into merging their worlds such that Ema and Pegasus would find their way to the Magic Forest and assist Annie and Big Bear in confounding yet another evil plot by the Bad Witch, and a couple of those became epics, lasting forty minutes or more, and afterward I was exhausted and required a glass of whiskey and a solid hour of cable news.

The traditional distracted father, the kind who regards his children from a safe physical and psychic distance, the kind who basically subcontracts the raising of children to his spouse, and simply sits at the center of his household as a fount of authority and abstract values, as God Almighty's gendered representative within the family unit, can never be an animal, and is rather a kind of troll for being constitutionally unable to humble himself to the will and ego requirements of children. Becoming an animal, one wholly domesticated to the messy, organic process of children's ego development, is indeed humbling, and is only possible when the classic lines of patriarchal authority are subverted. Bruno Bettelheim's famous study of fairytales, *The Uses of Enchantment*, does not directly account for original narratives, for the customized narratives, if you will, that a parent deploys out of love and knowledge of the child's immediate psychic circumstances, but his emphasis upon the profound usefulness of such entertainment is deeply true. We become animals not to replace the traditional narratives but to augment them.

My turning into animals for my daughters has not simply been a means of moral training (of course the most basic rules of human decency were and are the stories' subtext) and healthy ego development. From the beginning, I've feared losing my children to the Czech language and culture, to an extended family I can't offer them in America. I've feared someday seeming foreign to them. The stories were themselves (magic) islands of English during those months and years my daughters were otherwise immersed in Czech. My girls' contact with me was also contact with English, with America, with my home, my culture. Pegasus may have been born in ancient Greece but he became over the centuries a thoroughly American flying horse. Annie doesn't know it, but Big Bear and the Magic Forest are somewhere in northern California.

There's only so much a girl can do in a fairy grotto, but that is where Annie must spend at least a third of each visit. This means she spends two thirds of each story solving a problem or fixing a disaster, and then languishes, as a kind of reward, in the fairy grotto eating ambrosia and drinking nectar (the former being the most delicious pudding-like substance imaginable, and the latter a drink rather like banana smoothie, but much, much better). There is a Fairy Queen who holds forth from a ridiculously large blossom, and all the fairies, about an inch tall, flash one or another primary color, so the place, when it's really rocking, is like a psychedelic toy store at Christmas.

And it rocks. The fairies party hardy. They fly past Annie after she has saved the Magic Forest and give her the tiniest butterfly kisses, thousands. And they all gorge on ambrosia and nectar, though there are no fat fairies, given that ambrosia has no fat, no sugars, no carbs, yet fills one up though never to the point of satiety. It's a good time rather like the one had at the end of that silliest *Star Wars* movie that ended in a forest. That party, though, ended mercifully with the happy dead glowing and smiling and those little furry forest creatures dancing on tree limbs. That is, the party ended when the movie ended. The party in the Magic Forest is endless, and I must come up with new ways of presenting the same frivolity again and again. Sometimes, there are special games Annie plays, riding her broomstick Amelia, with the fairies; sometimes something disruptive happens in the midst of the partying, but that just means that Annie gets a two-fer, that I must churn out yet another plot, which will simply end up back in the Fairy Grotto, in the midst of a raging, endless party.

Indeed, some girls just want to have fun, especially fairies, and, though the Fairy Queen bears no resemblance to Paris Hilton, she seems driven by a similar social imperative to keep the party going. And does this mean Annie will drive me crazy in a few years by frequenting real-life party sites where a more erotic agenda than thousands of tiny butterfly kisses will prevail? Probably. But though I will not presume to be Big Bear waiting on the other side of the hedge, like a personal bodyguard who chats with the bouncers at the door, Big Bear, I hope, will indeed be waiting at the door of all menace, all dubious choices, never interfering, never presuming to insert himself between a young woman and her adventures, but there all the same, enabling, ready, when she is ready, to carry her back to the Old Oak Tree.

Storytelling and parenting are related joys often at cross-purposes. At an age when many of my writer friends are finishing their parenting duties and turning their full attention to their writing, I cannot see a time when I may do likewise. I mean, I simply cannot credibly project that far into the future. The imperative to become animals for my daughters will extend well into another decade, when my youngest daughter will need it most, especially given that she is favoring Czech over English to a much greater extent than did her sisters at the same age, and will therefore require even more stories.

I make no great claims for the stories I concoct for my children. They are sometimes "lame," as Annie often judges, and I often repeat plot points, and both of my daughters over the years have had to stop me mid yarn, pointing out that certain conditions in their respective magical worlds have changed by virtue of some cosmic event that occurred twenty or thirty stories ago (I forgot, the other evening, that the moon over the Magic Forest had turned crimson several months ago, though for the life of me I cannot recall how or why; surely I was thinking snidely of Revelations). Though I will make this claim: I'm a better writer for having told my girls so many stories just for them. I'm certainly not claiming even to be a good writer, just better than I would have been, and I think it's the "just for them" that has resulted in this condition.

Writing, presuming to make art, is an intrinsically selfish activity. Only a fool believes that her poems, fictions, or essays will make the world a truly better place. Of course, collectively, writers and writing improve the world in ways too richly complex even to touch on here, but taken book by book, story by story, not even the wisest, most soulful and thought-provoking creative effort resonates much beyond the dwindling tribe of sophisticated readers. Given that creative writing is more ego-driven than other human activities—business, athletics, even politics—it is a grand paradox that the value of "serious literature" is in its complex collective effect, not in the individual efforts composing that effect. Business and political leaders of course may be megalomaniacs, yet none may presume to have achieved her or his successes alone; only artists may, and only artists whose materials are language, the very coin of the realm of the ego, the very substance of human identity, may see themselves reflected in their creative activities and achievements to the extent that writers do.

Every writer—pedestrian, good, or great—must achieve an intimate relationship with an audience that largely doesn't exist. By "largely" I mean that there is a measurable audience for a relatively tiny percentage of even the truly excellent writing produced. That intimacy then is part chimera, part ego projection. It is a kind of madness, the kind that once was associated with divinity, with the transformative power of the divine.

The intimacy that I achieve with my daughters in the act of storytelling is akin to that which I assume in composing stories, poems and essays. Their profound presence as my audience has enabled me to achieve a deeper sense of intimacy when I write for my invisible, inaudible, (largely) nonexistent audience. When I become "poet" or "novelist" or "essayist" I transform into a no less ridiculous, wondrous creature than the horse, bear, or monkey I become for my girls. And, at this stage of my life and career, the transformation, though no less ego-driven than when I was a young poet, a young writer, has much more to do with love than it ever did before.

A Brief History of My Heart

WHEN I TELL MY DAUGHTERS I love them, I used to assume there is no ambiguity in the assertion. I long assumed that my love of my daughters is simple and profound even as my love of women, over the course of my life, has been everything but simple, and that the only profundity I may claim for my heart's quixotic journey through youth and beyond is a formidable capacity for self-deception. The fact of the matter is that my assumption of a bifurcated heart, one half dedicated to a pure love of daughters and the other to a richly complex and impure, which is to say sexually driven, love of women over a lifetime, has been false. I've been no less self-deceived in my love of my daughters than I have been, generally, in my erotic intimacies.

Early on, such self-deception enabled me to be a slut. In this, I was like almost everyone else I knew in San Diego in the early and mid-1970s, and now make no grand claims for my shenanigans. I was not a sterling rogue. I was just a run-of-the-mill, minor male slut. I was tall and skinny and had long, luxurious hair. I was sort of pretty, in a goofy way. Females liked me, did not find me threatening, and many attractive young women with little prodding had sex with me.

It is common wisdom that promiscuity is less sexual appetite than neurosis, though I must say that as a young man I had exquisite fun feeding my neuroses. I didn't hurt anyone, didn't lie, well, didn't lie much, and on the few occasions I told women I loved them I thought I meant it. Perhaps I did, but only the way a narcissist can, and all pretty young men, straight and gay, powered by that neurosis gadget hotwired to their psyches, are narcissists. Any such creature gazes into his own eyes reflected in the charmed eyes of a beloved and says, "I love you."

That fun-loving narcissist is forgivable. He'd survived a weird, unsettled childhood in which he'd too often had to assume the emotional gravity of an adult, so a protracted adolescence of benign promiscuity was, in some cosmic sense, only fair. But I transitioned out of that phase into one of failed serial monogamy: I cheated in both of my first two marriages; indeed, had I not cheated on my first wife with the woman who would become my second, I'd not have my three daughters.

As it is, my girls have a pretty good knowledge of the history of my heart. They know I was married before I married their mother. They know my first wife is named Betty and that she was a ballerina. They know Betty and I lived in the French Quarter, then moved to the Ninth Ward. They know Betty and I had a little fluffy dog and that Betty was beautiful and I loved her. They also know that their mother got pregnant with Ema while I was still married to Betty, and that I broke Betty's heart even as leaving her broke mine. They know, therefore, that though I have been kind to women, I have left them. I left Betty. I left their faux aunt who had been my mistress for most of my marriage to their mother. They know that, in a sense, I left their mother.

Though, I didn't really leave her. Their mother and I left each other; in fact she left first, but to say so may be putting too fine a point on the matter. What's important is that they know I will never leave them. They are certain I am a rock for them, and otherwise an excellent example of why, with rare exception, no woman should give all of herself to any man.

My daughters live with me for half of each year, the other half in Prague with their mother, though I spend at least two months each cycle in Prague working with and helping their mother. In a recent year, as the girls were in Prague and I was a visiting professor in southern California, I gave myself permission to regress, to become again that promiscuous hound I'd been three decades earlier. This regression, though, was mediated by the fact that I'm no longer pretty and no longer innocent. More importantly, even though my girls were not with me in the flesh, they occupied my psyche. I could not turn off my father self.

Yet I felt a powerful urge to open myself once more to multiple physical intimacies, and the result of following that urge was a series of tepid one-night stands and three more or less serious if mercifully brief relationships. The most significant common feature of those contacts was that they were all with women whose personalities were tempered by abuse.

There is no more evil act than an adult's defilement of a child. Where does such desire reside? Certainly not in the part of a person that wants to protect, as every true adult should feel compelled to do.

It must certainly be the case that such a person is not a true adult; he or she is disfigured to the core. Such an individual is rendered disfigured by putrid desires, but what part of a person does such desire inhabit? What causes that kind of desire? How can an adult feel sexual desire for any child, much less his own?

To most sophisticated folks, these questions may seem pathologically naïve. I've read studies documenting and explaining sexual abuse, I've listened for hours to female as well as male friends who have been victims, but nothing truly explains it. A dear, brilliant friend recently suggested that my not comprehending how a person may experience such desires is a blind spot of the imagination. My friend is much brighter and wiser than I, and I could only accept, with humility, her judgment. My imagination fails me, fails me utterly, regarding the defilement of children.

In each of those three relationships I wanted to help a woman heal from her inner torment, the memory of what had happened to her. One in particular had been so heinously defiled that when the full revelation of what had happened to her emerged, I felt gobsmacked. I wept. I confused pity with love, at least briefly.

The question of course is why was I drawn to those particular women at that time of my life. Or, more to the point, why were they drawn to me? All three were physically lovely, relatively successful. All three controlled, if tenuously, their pain, and all three were clearly tormented despite years of therapy in which they'd acquired what may only be called, I think, practical skills in managing sorrow.

The one I've characterized as most heinously defiled broke my heart, which is simply to say that I learned that her attraction for me was the result, primarily, of viewing me from afar interacting at public events with my daughters, and through the early, intense stages of our sexual relationship, I learned first that she'd been abused, but then, slowly, inexorably, I learned of the duration and horror of that abuse.

At one point, she accused me of dredging the horror out of her, of compelling her to relive it after years of existing, in some precarious sense, beyond it. The fact was that I simply asked questions any caring lover should, answers led to further questions, and the momentum of her revelations became a sad cascade in the dark between us.

I wanted to help her heal, even as I realized, also slowly, that I could never let her near my daughters. Though she was gentle and composed on the surface, her sickness regarding the very category, "daughter," seemed like a kind of quicksand visible not far ahead.

In the history of my heart, I've healed no one. I've been true to three girls, have fed them, bathed them when they were infants, read endlessly to them, talked to them endlessly, listened to them chatter, listened to them rage and weep and howl with joy. In the history of my heart I have loved incredible women imperfectly, sometimes poorly, but I have been true to my daughters as I was not true even to my mother.

When my mother grew ill, my father was in prison for the second time. She and we five children lived in the Norfolk projects and collected welfare. When she was finally diagnosed with multiple sclerosis, she said, "At least now I know what's killing me."

During the period when her despair was deepest, right after her lover left, she pregnant, and weeks before my father was to be released from prison and, that first night with us, would punch her in the stomach to cause a miscarriage, I would lie in her bed and try to make her laugh, try to make her talk about happy stuff. My brothers and sister would be sleeping. She'd smoke Pall Malls and chatter, sometimes suddenly sob then compose herself and continue whatever story about her girlhood she'd been telling. I'd fetch her glasses of water from the bathroom tap and empty her ashtray, and when she had to rise to go to the bathroom, I'd let her use me as a walking stick; I'd wait at the door until she finished peeing, and let her press her hand into my shoulder to keep balance back to the bed.

I was twelve. Masturbation had supplanted basketball as my favorite sport. I knew my mother was pregnant with Joey's child. She'd come into my room weeping one night, woke me, and told me she was pregnant and that Joey, a sailor whom I quite liked, had to leave us.

I knew that my mother was pregnant and in all likelihood dying. I spent every waking hour fantasizing about naked females, but not when I was with her. In her bed, I focused on her, listened, in the dark, to her stories, asked her to sing. She would sometimes sing "Soft as the Voice of an Angel," or "I'm Looking Over a Four-Leaf Clover." Her voice was pretty but raspy from cigarettes.

I wanted nothing more than for her to be well and happy. I was twelve and transforming out of childhood, and the woman from whose body I'd issued was suffering, trapped, dying in the dark beside me. The red tip of her cigarette arced upon the darkness of that room, and she stared at the shadows on the ceiling and told me stories about her brothers and about growing up in Norfolk during the Depression and the Second World War, about how she was featured on the cover of *Navy Times* as a "Norfolk beauty," and how she sang "I'm Looking Over a Four Leaf Clover" on a local TV show just before she met my father. She was a local beauty who sang on TV; surely a better life would have been possible. I remember even saying that if she hadn't met my father her life would have been so much better, and she said, but then she wouldn't have had me. Still, less than a year later I was offered the choice of staying with her or being adopted by relatives and taken to Sasebo, Japan. I was thirteen, and never should have been given such a choice. I chose to leave her.

Why those women chose me—and it was indeed they who chose; I've so often been clueless as to who indeed was driving the intimacy agenda—I can't really know, though I have to think it had something to do, as was true when I was a promiscuous young man, with my not seeming a threat. That all three relations were awkward and, finally, inappropriate, became clear soon enough, though barely soon enough.

Returning from an eight-day liaison in a tree-pretty, late-summer rustic place with the third of my damaged lovers, I was emotionally spent, and a little ashamed that I'd allowed myself a year of false intimacies, false in the sense that I'd known in each case the woman's isolation was a condition of her calm, her daily passage among others. Each, heroic in her way, as are all victims of abuse who manage to push on along a path that does not lead to ruin, desired a few moments of friendship, sex, or drama, but did not require or desire anything like commitment. And as had been the case when I was a goofy young rogue, I wasn't prepared to offer much more than a little fun, a little diversion. Had they or I derived anything substantial from our contacts? At least my pathology of rescue and abandonment had played out; at least I'd recognized a pattern.

But the simple truth of my relations to females over time is that becoming a father changed my heart. It's not that my heart is bifurcated, one half pure in its regard for four particular females, my dead mother and three living daughters, and in the other roiled by sexual desire and repulsion. Rather, it is simply and pro-foundly changed. Now, in my heart, every female is a daughter, if not mine then someone's, and I am now incapable of regarding any woman with whom I forge a personal or professional relationship, no matter her age, except as a daughter, someone to be respected and nurtured, someone to be listened to, someone, alas, to be protected, and of course it is in this final aspect, good intentions notwithstanding, that the age-old patriarchal agenda hunkers down. Especially regarding daughters, it is every father's moral imperative, in such a world as this, to protect without controlling, never to put a female in a position where she must barter freedom for protection, in either a physical or psychological sense.

I speak now from the first weeks of a third marriage. Whereas my first union was capricious, my second compelled by circumstances, this one occurs in the midst of a quiet acceptance of mortality and the stark necessities of that singular fact. My mate survived the emotional abuse of a sick, rich, and powerful first husband, but is no one's victim; her capacity for joy seems often otherworldly. I've told her the history of my heart, not this truncated, public one but the long story one voices in the dark, on both sides of lovemaking, both sides of sleep, the story of self-deceptions and good intentions; the true story of hope and failed intimacies; the story of false steps and missed connections. It is the story of cowardly, though often comical, wincing away from the full-blooded needs of good women who deserved better and have, for the most part, achieved it in the wake of my presence in their lives.

It is a cautionary tale to all daughters, that is, all women, and it is one I've told but once, and only to my beloved, though I've also told it, pieces of it, anyway, in the scattered narratives composing my "life's work."

"True love" and artistic ambition are not so much at odds as mutually corrupting, but only perniciously so, I think, when love is not understood to be a choice. When love is not a choice, it is a sickness. Suffice it to say that a brief history of each of our hearts, men and women, straight, gay, and lesbian, will have a beginning, a middle, but no end that will not read like yet another beginning.

If histories are written by the victorious, they may also be contrived by the self-defeated. And isn't it the case that at one time or another we are all self-defeated in matters of the heart, those diversions from mortality that are the very essence of mortality? In the heart, Good Intentions march lockstep through the grand twin columns of I Love You and I'm Leaving You. They march on a vast boulevard which circles the city. They march and they march, that army of Good Intentions, where there is nothing to engage, nothing to defeat or be defeated by. True love is as radical a choice as whether to live or cease living.

Scorpio Rising: How I Found the Title for my Selected Poems

I DROVE MY TWO YOUNGER DAUGHTERS, Annie and Ellie, with my wife Krista, from Kalamazoo, Michigan, where we live (the girls six months with us, the rest of the year in Prague with their mother) to the amusement park in Cedar Point, Ohio. It's a three and a half-hour journey through some of America's more numbing landscape. The Prague Summer Program, which I directed in partnership with my daughters' Czech mother for sixteen years, had ended three weeks earlier, and we were having a mid-August American fling before school would begin after Labor Day.

Cedar Point amusement park is awesome in the original sense of being both impressive and—at least in terms of pop-cultural resonance—frightening. Its titanium and plastic magnitude, its glorious monotony of blurred primary colors and epic queues, of adrenaline rush in one hundred-degree swelter, had much more to do with endurance than amusement.

And even if the lines had been briefer and the weather more pleasant, my experience of that dizzying enclave would still have been a mere matter of endurance, except that my girls were fully engaged, and except that Krista possesses an uncanny gift for accompanying the girls on their adventures far beyond my jaded purview. My twelve-year-old Annie and I shuffled for eighty minutes in a winding queue, occasionally misted by industrial fans, until it was our turn to get strapped into a "drag racer" that accelerated from zero to one hundred and twenty in four seconds, shot three hundred feet into the sky and looped down, twisting twice before delivering us to where we began, in eleven seconds. Such is life's ratio of anticipation to actualization. Our final ride, at dusk, eleven hours after we'd entered the massive park, was on an old-school wooden roller coaster dubbed "Wicked Twister." Annie and I, at her insistence because she'd already ridden the thing twice with Krista, occupied the last car. She knew from experience that the final unit shook more violently than the others, and delighted in my discomfort. I am muscular and paunchy-large, and do not take such action well. Exiting the caboose, I felt as though my kidneys had dislodged from their moorings.

The night before, we occupied two double beds a couple miles from the Cedar Point compound. Krista slept with Annie farthest from the door and window, I with four and a half-year-old Ellie closest to the wall unit that groaned all night to cool us. I'd been thinking for days about my Selected, about my relation to poetry, about my "career."

I awoke at four in the morning, an hour earlier than I usually do, and, of course, felt pinned to the sheets because I didn't want to waken my family. I lay, trying to conjure a title. I ticked through all of the pithy, memorable (I could only hope) turns of phrase from my six poetry collections. It was rather like spinning through the alphabet again and again, trying to grapple a famous name I was a little terrified at not recalling.

However, in a calm moment of relenting, of giving up the casting of one hooked letter after another into the bleak waters of my recall, "Scorpio Rising" whispered into me.

Okay, this sounds incredibly self-indulgent, I know, but I'm sure that all of us who write, all of us who aspire to make art of any kind, have received such a gift, perhaps many times, or feel that we have. Where did this particular gift originate?

I'd married Krista but eight months earlier, after a whirlwind courtship. We'd known each other casually for eight years, but our contact over most of that time had been scattered and brief. We conducted our love affair as improbable newlyweds and in the midst of much frenetic and passionate parenting. Of course, after accepting my marriage proposal, Krista had the daunting task of winning the hearts of three young, worldly, and skeptical Czech-American females, not to mention their worldly and skeptical Czech mother. Luckily, Krista is irresistibly charming, and charmingly genuine, in every sense.

She is also someone who takes astrology seriously. I never did. I'd regarded it as I do organized religion, as a salve for the terror of extinction. The only hocus pocus I'd ever been able to acknowledge was the question mark at the heart of existence.

Krista says she never thought she'd "end up" with a Scorpio, and often lists the features of the sign that fit, to her mind perfectly, my character and personality. She views me as a classic Scorpio, so when we decided, in Prague, to add to our menagerie of tattoos (she has seven, I four), I chose an image of a scorpion for my right outer forearm.

As I lay in that motel bed, ruing the day to come even as I relished it for the love of my family, "Scorpio Rising" wafted from that mucky cauldron of my unconscious, and I did what most of us would do; I rose gingerly from that bed, first plucking Ellie's leg from my own and tucking the blanket back around her, and, fetching my laptop, sat at the little table that was littered with the stuff of family travel, and Googled "Scorpio Rising." Sitting atop the astrological chatter was something remarkable.

The groan of the AC, before which I perched taking its cool blast full on, filled my head, so I flicked it off. Bodies shifted in the new quiet as I learned that *Scorpio Rising* is the title of a 1964, twenty-eight-minute art flick by Kenneth Anger. A major precursor of the music videos that would flicker on our cave walls fifteen years or so later, it's technically primitive and conceptually brilliant. The soundtrack has no dialogue, only popular songs of the period ("Fools Rush In," "My Boyfriend's Back," "Blue Velvet," "Devil in Disguise," "Hit the Road Jack," "Heat Wave," "I Will Follow Him," and "Wipe Out" most memorably). As I viewed the black-and-white film on YouTube, I had to keep the sound down and an ear close to the speaker so as not to awaken Krista and the girls. I'm a little ashamed to admit that though I'd heard of Anger in connection with his cheesy occult interests that included a casual relation to Charles Manson, I'd never heard of *Scorpio Rising*, in fact had never seen any of his films.

Mega-campy images of beautiful young leather men gunning glorious hogs are interspersed with scenes from a Jesus flick, *The Greatest Story Ever Told*, I think, and with flashes of swastikas and other iconic Nazi images. One of the composition's themes is deconstructed masculinity. Jesus and his disciples were indeed a kind of homoerotic proto biker club, and that Nazism was sado-masochistic I suppose today goes without saying; most bright folks who'd grown up during the war, as Anger had, and who'd digested even a smidgen of Freud, understood Nazism's hyper-masculine drag show to be all about homoerotic sadomasochism, basically, sticking it to one's subordinates, as well as one's enemies, right down the line.

When my father got out of the federal penitentiary in Harrisburg, Pennsylvania, he'd gained thirty pounds of muscle and a scowl that never faded. He was utterly transformed. The handsome, goofy, fun-loving criminal I'd adored as a young child had changed into a monster. Soon after the Cuban Missile Crisis, we hit the road again, spending several weeks in Hawaii, before he was caught and put back in prison. Once more we lived on welfare, this time in the Norfolk housing projects. My mother contracted multiple sclerosis, my father got out of prison in the fall, I think, of 1966, and by the early spring of 1967, I and my brother, two years younger than I, were adopted by relatives we'd never known and whisked off to Sasebo, Japan, where our new stepfather, a low-ranking naval officer, was the skipper of a coastal mine sweeper. He was deeply decent and mostly absent. In Sasebo, I earned a second-degree black belt in Shobukan Okinawa-te.

Like many young males, I sought fathers through adolescence and well into adulthood. That I sought them, in part, to kill them I did not fully realize until long past the period of my impassioned search. I found my psyche's fathers primarily in the tribe of poets, and it was indeed masculine American poets I sought to emulate and, figuratively, to kill. Philip Levine, Galway Kinnell, Robert Bly, James Dickey, Mark Strand, Donald Justice, Robert Mezey, Richard Hugo, James Wright, Louis Simpson, William Stafford, Gerald Stern, and Richard Wilbur were chief among them. Some of these fathers I came to know, a few I met casually, and a couple, William Stafford and James Wright, I never had the privilege of meeting.

From early on, I knew that my subject as a poet was manhood, how to be a man. And, of course, as a result of the probing and prodding of hermeneutics ranging from classic feminism to queer theory, the categories "manhood" and "man," over the course of my adult life, my intellectual and emotional development, have been, at the very least, problematic. Hemingway, Miller, Mailer and so many others had already been hoisted with their own petards by the time I'd realized my subject.

My father taught me, from the time I was able to answer him from the backseat of a stolen automobile, that physical courage trumps every other human quality. To be a man, by his reckoning, was quite simply to face physical danger, usually in the form of conflict with another male, and to take a beating stoically or likewise to administer one.

I experienced deep shame as a boy, both times my father was in prison, whenever I felt fear. Hopping trains and riding them, across trestles, across two hundred-foot drops—shallow, rocky creeks—was terrifying, but I couldn't choose not to do so. Not risking my life after other guys had risked theirs was not an option; I literally could not imagine turning away, not taking a challenge. When a larger boy threatened me, I didn't ever have the option of running. I fought all comers. My father, from his jail cell, compelled me. Not living up to his mandate of manhood was my only mortification. I mean, it was not simply an issue of what I did; I fought when I had to fight and performed incredibly stupid death-defying acts when challenged. That I felt fear at all was my shame. My father not only compelled my actions from his jail cell; he reached from there into my heart.

Of course, this is pretty tame stuff. It is quite likely that many of the older boys I fought and followed in the poor neighborhoods of Elizabeth City and Norfolk, older boys I challenged and was challenged by, went to Vietnam. I didn't. My lottery number was 339 in 1972, a year when I'd not likely have been drafted even if my number had been a single digit. But I was terrified of being drafted, being sent to Nam and getting killed, though as I sat before the radio with my compatriots in Coronado, California, all of us born in 1953, I was the badass, the skinny, goofy guy who "knew" karate, who taught it for a partial living. I was the guy everyone liked okay but knew not to fuck with. They'd seen me break rocks and bricks with the ridge of my right hand at keg parties. They'd seen me fight in fast-food parking lots. There were stories about me taking out two sailors in the Greasy Spoon on Orange Avenue. My reputation was perhaps eighteen percent deserved.

In 1976, a guy who'd picked me up hitchhiking south of Dallas woke me up and told me to get out of his little truck. I'd heard of the French Quarter, recalled that the previous evening the guy had told me the French Quarter would be the end of the road. As I'd drifted off, I'd recalled that I had a buddy, Bernie Gallant, who lived and worked there in the Chart House Restaurant. Public phones were a nickel. By that evening I was scrubbing pots and banging racks of dirty platters into a dishwasher.

From the mid-seventies to the mid-eighties, the French Quarter was a decisively gay community; straights who lived there felt as though they were being allowed to, at least I did, and I was grateful. Soon after taking up employment at the Chart House, I met the woman I would live with in her apartment on Dumaine and eventually, ludicrously, marry. After my adventures in three graduate programs, interspersed with gigs at several French Quarter upscale restaurants, Betty and I moved into what our landlord insisted, on one occasion swore, was the original House of the Rising Sun, on Saint Louis between Bourbon and Dauphine, across the street from Al Hirt, or "Jumbo" as he insisted we call him.

Betty, a gorgeous and deeply good person, was what we called, with no disparagement, a fag hag. Gay men flocked to her, and in the French Quarter, in the late seventies and early eighties, the flock was huge. If I desired, for example, to spend time with her on those rare occasions neither she nor I worked a weekend, or if I desired simply to party with her into the wee hours after our shifts, which typically ended after midnight, I had to accommodate myself to her gay gang. I was tolerated by some, welcomed by others, but all and all was accepted, if warily, as Betty's straight guy.

So, through most of my twenties, I witnessed, lived in the midst of, Southern Camp culture, and was no doubt influenced by it in ways that I probably still don't fully understand. What I do understand, what I recall so vividly, is the effect of the AIDS plague on the French Quarter beginning around 1980, accelerating through the early eighties. There were many deaths, much mourning those years, much despair, though Betty and I kept all that death on the periphery. We were happy, in a fashion, in our House of the Rising Sun.

How I got from New Orleans to Prague, and as a result to fatherhood, is a goofy tale I've told elsewhere. Suffice it to say that being a father of females, and for a time a single parent for half of each year, has required that I stare deeply into a sense of manhood mitigated by camp culture and generally picked apart by a range of critiques. My lyric poems, I hope among other things, chronicle my shifting conception of my own gendered identity, particularly regarding my roles as teacher, friend, father, lover, tourist/witness, and citizen.

Whether or not I'm ever able to write verse again, I feel deeply blessed to have been admitted to the tribe of American poets as a young man. At the risk of sounding maudlin, I wish to say here: I love poetry, particularly when I teach it, and I love my mother and father, brother and sister poets. If I'd not found poetry, or if it hadn't found me, I'd probably have ended up in prison. My Scorpio nature (as my New Age mate describes it to me), my weird childhood, would have led me there, to that horror, to that particular version of manhood.

Strapped and wedged into that last car of Wicked Twister with my beautiful daughter, as the linked cars clicked slowly upward toward the first horrendous drop, I watched lights snap on all over the park, and commented to my girl how beautiful they were in such a crystalline twilight, but she cared for nothing that moment but the clicks of our rising, was fixed solely on the anticipation of our first thrilling plunge, and I loved my life.

The Magic Book:
Why I Thought Publishing
a Book Would Change Everything

ONE BRISK SATURDAY MORNING, IN NORFOLK, Virginia, mid-autumn 1965, I wandered through the parking lot of the Giant Open Air Super Market, a few blocks from the projects. I wore a tattered black leather jacket I'd procured from the local Salvation Army church, where my family acquired all of our clothes. It just so happened that the Salvation Army was conducting a used-book sale in that parking lot, and, without thinking, I grabbed two books from one of many piles, lined up on folding card tables at the rear of the lot, and ran like hell. I was more than halfway back to the projects when I pulled up, gasping, and studied what I'd filched, stolen for no other reason than the thrill of doing so. Both, ironically, I would notice years later, were Taiwanese pirated editions: Louis Untermeyer's *A Treasury of Great Poems* and *The Complete Poems of Robert Frost*.

What if I'd stolen books about high finance, architecture, or landscape gardening? Would my life have taken a different path? Would high finance, architecture, or landscape gardening have saved my life? I don't know, but I doubt it. I think I'd have found poetry one way or another. I think that one way or another I'd have found my poet fathers to slay and poet mothers to long for.

I'd have found my poet brothers and sisters, my tribe, my spiritual home. But that moment of puzzling over those books, as I stood beside the huge drainage ditch between Comstock's Drug Store, where I bought and stole my DC and Marvel comics, and the projects where I lived, I knew I held in my hands something truly marvelous. I'm not sure I'd ever even seen a "poem," words lined up like *that*, words sounding like *that*. At first, as I read randomly and shuffled homeward, I was puzzled yet intrigued. I would soon fall in love with those books and seek others. Poetry was my secret for years. Within months of that same year, I somehow got my hands on *A Coney Island of the Mind* and, so, poetry closer to my urban experience, and something gloriously tainted by popular culture, became available. I "understood" so little of the poetry I read as a boy, but I wasn't bothered by incomprehension. I took it in stride, even relished it, the mystery of what I could not fathom in poetry.

At the age of twenty-nine, in the early autumn of 1983, my first year living in the House of the Rising Sun in the French Quarter of New Orleans, I received in the mail the package containing two hardback copies of my first book, *Green Dragons*, winner of the Wesleyan University Press New Poets Series. I can look back now over the almost thirty years and realize how silly I was as I ripped the envelope open and held my book, gazed into the image on the dust jacket with a soulful intensity I'd never felt before, and would not feel again until eight years later when I'd gaze into the crinkled face of my swaddled newborn first daughter.

I'm certain that every published writer can tell a similar story of that first moment of clutching that first book, turning it over again and again in one's hands, opening it and flipping rapidly through the pages, lifting it to one's face and breathing it in, all but inhaling it, indeed all but eating it, of feeling that the thing is magic, will magically transform human existence. That feeling is a narcissistic idiocy that soon passes, or at least ratchets down in intensity. And at some point one feels, at least I do, a kind of shame for having been so self-consumed, for having invested so much ego in such a simple, even humble object.

As one reaches the point when Peggy Lee's "Is That All There Is" becomes something like the National Anthem of the Inner Life, of course all the remembered manifestations of youthful narcissism become a source of great shame, and yet such shame is not the same as regret. I can never regret feeling so marvelous as I did holding in my hands for the first time my first book. I did not yet fully fathom how lucky I was not to be in prison or swabbing the deck of an aircraft carrier; nor did I yet fully fathom how blessed I was to have published a first book with such a prestigious press. A decade earlier I'd moseyed, my nerves sparking, through the Coronado Public Library, coming down from half a hit of Windowpane, and spied three thin books at odd angles on a table in the stacks. I paused to touch them and read the titles: *Not This Pig* by Philip Levine, *Saint Judas* by James Wright, and *Helmets* by James Dickey. Wesleyan University Press had published all three, though at the time I didn't notice such things. At nineteen I fancied myself a poet, would get stoned and listen to LP's, in the tiny booths of that library, of Dylan Thomas declaiming "Fern Hill" and T. S. Eliot "The Hollow Men." But, with the exceptions of Ferlinghetti and Ginsberg, I hadn't read any contemporary poetry. Feeling as though I had battery cables clamped to my ears and someone was revving the engine, I sat at that table and read those books, and when I'd finished reading every single word of all three, I felt gobsmacked, transformed. A window was opened, and I crawled through, and the first thing I saw on the other side, ten years later, was a little book with my name on it. The fact that my moment of narcissistic glory was tethered to the wonder I first felt as a thieving boy, and that that wonder coalesced into an all but selfless love for those qualities of affection and vision and truth telling that I first encountered as a nineteen-year-old kid in a library on acid, renders my self-congratulatory moment of utter self-consumption forgivable. That is, I forgive myself for having been so happy that moment I held my first book, and for being so happy about it for so long after. I was probably insufferable to my new colleagues, especially my fellow junior faculty who had not yet published books. I was probably insufferable not because I bragged or passed among them with a swagger, but because I was so happy. I'd spent the last decade climbing through a window, and I was finally on the other side.

But where was that?

Who has roamed through a university or big-city library and not felt profoundly humbled? Who has not contemplated the sheer volume of information contained in books, the unfathomable range of information, and not felt infinitesimal? What information did my first little book contain? What information have any of my little books contained? Well, mostly info about me, how and what I've thought and felt over a range of circumstances. Hardly world-rocking stuff. Whitman yelped, "Who touches this book touches a man!" and the floodgates were opened to a century and a half of ego-spew, Romantic self-consciousness with an American zest, a radical egalitarianism that is uniquely American.

It took me ten years to climb through a window, and once I was on the other side it took me a long time to realize that I'd not climbed out but rather in. I'd broken into the House of Art, but not to burgle, not to snatch, bag, and escape. I was there, remain there, because outside is pain and despair. Outside, suicide is an option, and love is only chemistry.

Holding my little book almost thirty years ago, I held my own life, my life affirmed, my life transformed from lead into gold, or shiny copper at least. I became a published author; my name was surely destined to become a household word in dozens of homes across America! I was skinny and kind of pretty back then. I had one chin, so did not require facial hair. I gave readings to promote my little book, and actually sold a goodly number. During readings, I'd stare into my book, glancing up to make fake eye contact every few seconds. My "reading" was really a recitation, because I had the whole book memorized. Above all, I wanted the women in the audiences to like me. I gave readings at colleges and universities that never would have admitted me had I applied to them. I was a young man telling his life story in ragged verses. Many of my poems were about the suffering of others: my family; hookers in Sasebo, Japan; doomed Marines on their way to Vietnam; wretched winos passed out on gas-lit French Quarter stoops; young gay men desperate for love on the balcony of Laffite in Exile; I referenced their sadness, their suffering, with a goofy joy. Though I'd composed the poems of *Green Dragons* in a state of empathy, I performed them, gazing into the book, a commodity of which the supply far exceeded the demand, full of pride in that object, that fetish, that catalyst to my transformation, that prize I'd climbed through a magic window to acquire, the very source of that magic that had opened the window, had placed the open window in my path.

Well, we soon learn that all textuality is intertextuality, and we learn as well that there is no author, not really. There is only what

Foucault termed "the author function." I hadn't yet begun my decade-long autodidact's foray into cultural and literary theory and criticism, so on the occasion of gazing into my first book I assumed it was all *mine*, that every word *belonged to me*.

In fact, somewhere a tree had fallen in a forest, and whether or not anyone had been present to see and hear it fall, it was eventually processed into paper, and those pages were spattered with ink arranged into shapes that were letters I'd pressed into patterns, grammatical units forming sentences, my texts, my ragged verses. Whether it existed because I perceived it, or whether it and I were merely projections of the glorious mind of God, that moment I first held it I knew that I would never climb back through the window, out of the House of Art, a condition of heart and mind that does not require an occupant to compose and publish a book: it had simply required that *I* compose and publish one.

But what if I'd been born in 1993 rather than 1953? That Richard Katrovas will not turn twenty-nine until 2022. I imagine him receiving an e-mail congratulating him for being chosen, out of more than two thousand young poets, to have his book published online by a prestigious university press. It will be immediately available, of course, for downloading onto the ubiquitous electronic reading pads, and may still be available through print on demand, though, even in so relatively short a period of time, the book as a fetish, as a magical object, as a thing that an ego may attach to, be anchored or buoyed by, will likely be past. When that Richard Katrovas is my present age, the year will be 2048. Will the atrocious nostalgia that I'm invoking here be relevant to that writer's life? His first book will never, none of his books will ever, "go out of print"; they will always be available. Of course the Internet will by then be littered with tens of millions of poetry books, if it isn't already, but most of the ones that actually get read by discerning audiences will have been vetted by respected publishers, thoroughly peer reviewed, and this will be true of all types of texts.

So much of lyric expression is about loneliness. Reading, at its best, is an exquisitely lonely endeavor. As a kid in the projects, my old man in the joint and my mother dying, I read to escape in the most profound sense. We lived on 169 dollars a month from welfare, not a hell of a lot even in the mid-sixties, especially given that our rent was sixty a month. Our end of the projects, the white end, butted up against a lower middle-class neighborhood of black homeowners. I knocked on doors and asked if I could do odd jobs, even mow lawns with a crappy push mower I'd extracted from a junk heap. I'd earn a quarter to fifty cents mowing a lawn, and some Saturdays I'd earn as much as three dollars, more than half of which purchased comic books. (Among hundreds I'd collected, kept in the third drawer of a battered chest of five drawers, was *Daredevil* 1 through 8 in pristine condition. Oh that I had sealed just those eight in plastic, then encased that bundle in something enduring and buried it somewhere accessible though remote, I might return to the projects of Norfolk, Virginia, and exhume those comic books—which are neither "books" nor particularly funny—sell them on eBay and pay off my 2006 C-class Mercedes!) The exquisite loneliness of all pastoral expression and all passionate reading is simply that adolescent angst, which, if we're lucky, never withers wholly away. With a stack of new comics and my two filched books, I'd sit half-lotus in the little field across a dirt road from the left bank of the Elizabeth River, and give my life over to a summer day filled with that exquisite loneliness, that holy anonymity.

Well, I'm no longer anonymous in that same holy sense; indeed, I am ashamed to confess that I am an inveterate Googler of my own name, a form of mid-life onanism that may not cause blindness nor hair to sprout from one's palms, though perhaps the jury's still out regarding its long-term deleterious effects. Suffice it to say that a fair chunk of the items associated with my name that get dredged up by that omniscient search engine have to do with people trying to sell used copies of my books. Terse descriptions of the books are always included, such that I know a hardback copy of *Green Dragons* exists somewhere on this planet with only a coffee-cup ring marring the otherwise perfectly preserved original dust jacket.

There is no way to calculate the intrinsic value of any book. What value may we place upon a novel or collection of poems or work of history or philosophy or scholarly study, or comic book, even, which changes or sustains an individual's life? What confronts us now is the bifurcation of "book" along the conceptual fault line of content and form. We may now have access to the content of any book *sans* that very form or container which defines it. The extrinsic value of a book is purely a matter of market imperatives. I love it that the first poetry books I ever read were Taiwanese pirated editions, that international copyright lawbreakers, Chinese ones at that, had calculated that Untermeyer's anthology and Frost's collected might actually fetch some coin. I thought nothing of this as a kid, of course, but now I am mystified. Surely people who publish illegally are usually more savvy about product. Those books were illegally printed in the late fifties or early sixties. What in God's name were those Chinese people thinking?

I would be delighted if one of my poetry books were thus disseminated across Anglophone Asia. I would love it if my name were a household word in more than a dozen homes across America, even if there were no monetary compensation. It's not as though I have actually made a living as a writer up to this point.

Intrinsic and extrinsic values merge in the enterprise of book collecting. When the content of a book has achieved an unquantifiable though very real transcendent value in the hearts of a coterie, or in the larger culture, that book's "original" form may be assigned an extrinsic, dollar value. In other words, such books enter the realm of visual art and baseball cards.

To lessen the book-buying burden on my students, I often cobble together reading lists that are wholly, or almost wholly, accessible online. It is easy enough to download everything from *Huckleberry Finn* and "Bartleby, the Scrivener" to the poems and essays of T. S. Eliot onto one's laptop. Soon, virtually all the world's books will be virtual, accessible, if the content is newly published, for a small fee. Amazon will continue to trend toward the iTunes model, I suppose.

But my guess is that even as books become obsolete as the principle storage and delivery containers for verbal content, the physical book as an art object will enter a protracted period of renaissance. Authors will seek to have fine, limited editions even of their bestsellers produced by artisans. Indeed, to a much greater extent than is true today, many fine boutique printers, artists in their own right, will seek to print limited editions of the very best books in all fields, but especially in the literary arts. The best books will have two lives, in mass distribution, or at least mass accessibility, in the virtual world, but also in small fine editions for small discerning audiences of the writer's friends and loved ones, as well as inveterate book collectors, a category of human endeavor that will grow exponentially, but only up to a point.

On a flight home this spring from Prague, I met a couple of guys, roughly my age, who happened also to have Kalamazoo, Michigan, as a final destination. One of them was a colleague from another department at Western Michigan University whom I'd never met and may very well never see again. I chatted up the Prague Summer Program, which he vaguely recalled having heard mentioned. He talked about his Kindle, about subscribing to the likes of *Sports Illustrated*, and how the "cover" now features not a static photograph, but rather a video stream. "Just like Harry Potter!" he finished, chuckling.

My second daughter, fourteen, spends many hours on her computer, mostly on Facebook and on exclusively Czech-language social networking sites. When she is not exchanging cryptic, terse, misspelled messages with her posse of girls, her only other reading, usually, is of fashion and pop culture magazines. When we stand in line at the supermarket, in Prague or Kalamazoo, and she tosses a magazine on the pile of groceries, I will often pick up the magazine and page through it. My response is usually, "But, Annie, there's nothing here but pictures!" She'll protest that there's plenty of text, snatch the mag from my fingers, leaf through, and triumphantly point to a quarter column of print, a caption to a photograph in which Brangelina is hauling clingy children through an airport.

The blending of image and text, in which the text is secondary to image, certainly did not begin with the Internet. It is the very nature of print advertising, and I wonder if the graphic novel, high culture offspring of the comic book, will not in a generation supplant the traditional novel. The technology by which even a visual illiterate such as myself may produce vibrant, original, and complex images will surely be available. Indeed, the technology by which anyone may produce quite incredible cinemagraphic narratives will be available. Any schmuck will have the tools to out-James Cameron James Cameron. Isn't it the case that one of the reasons there are as many "writers" as there are today is because it's a cheap form of self-expression? When other more exotic forms of self-expression become not only available but also easy to access, won't there be a great migration toward such exotic forms of storytelling? The migration away from strictly verbal texts has, of course, already begun in the form of ever more complex and narratively rich video games, and some of the cheesiest science fiction has already pointed toward a world in which alternate, virtual "realities" will be available, presenting quite staggering moral and ethical issues. The very nature of human intimacy is the ultimate issue. I am not one who believes that Facebook is a flash in the pan; rather, I believe that it is just a primitive beginning.

"We are the degenerate descendants of fathers who in their turn were degenerate from their forebears," proclaimed Horace more than two thousand years ago, and this degeneracy is particularly true regarding memory. The great storytellers of prehistory committed vast language constructs to memory, and, so, many of the conventions of "traditional verse" are but vestiges of oral traditions, the mnemonic devices that facilitated memorization of—literally—epic proportions. Textuality in pre-literate cultural contexts is a matter of physical proximity, intimacy, even. The presence of at least one other human being is necessary for the aural exchange to occur. And what we may call oral traditions did not, do not exist within a simplistic, linear historical context. Clay tablets, papyrus, wax tablets, and parchment scrolls held records of practical and cultural information in the midst of thriving oral traditions. The illuminated texts emanating from the scriptoria of medieval monasteries were the rarefied products of isolated labor occurring in the midst of a bustling cultural life animated by folktales, superstition, and rumor, and likewise the more or less secular scriptoria that serviced the burgeoning university libraries of the twelfth, thirteenth, and fourteenth centuries. Even as Europe transitioned from manuscript culture to the printed book following Gutenberg's invention of the printing press mid-fifteenth century, the vast majority of people, through the Renaissance right onto the cusp of the nineteenth century, were not only unaffected by book culture but were illiterate. And even as we contemplate how truly rarefied authorship was as a social niche up until only a couple hundred years ago, it is also interesting to note that authorship only relatively recently began to convey authorial rights. For many centuries, any text could be copied and sold or otherwise disseminated with impunity. Authorship that occurred outside systems of patronage offered little more than unremunerated glory. Even as today we observe the music business transforming as a business, becoming increasingly more diffuse, less profitable, more ad hoc, less secure in its mechanisms of exchange, so the e-book industry, as it evolves, will surely return us to that era of unremunerated, or under-remunerated, glory.

In his famous essay "The Work of Art in the Age of Mechanical Reproduction," Walter Benjamin mourns the loss of "the aura," what he characterizes as the moment of awe experienced by an individual witnessing a work of art for the first time. He argues that commercialization has subjected "the aura" to a grotesque warping of value, and the result is a cheapened "cult value." Of course, his emphasis in this formulation is on visual art, and throughout his groundbreaking essay his focus, when looking back, is on the visual and plastic arts, and on photography, cinema, and performing arts generally when speculating about the future. However, I think that his formulation regarding "aura" is more broadly applicable to include the literary arts: in this sense, the manifestation of aura has less to do, I think, with that rarefied moment of discovery in the exchange between an "original" work of visual art and a discerning witness than with the very nature of the relationship between "author" and consumer of language texts. Quoting Benjamin:

> *For centuries a small number of writers were confronted by many thousands of readers. This changed toward the end of the last century. With the increasing extension of the press, which kept placing new political, religious, scientific, professional, and local organs before the readers, an increasing number of readers became writers—at first, occasional ones. It began with the daily press opening to its readers space for "letters to the editor." And today there is hardly a gainfully employed European who could not, in principle, find an opportunity to publish somewhere or other comments on his work, grievances, documentary reports, or that sort of thing. Thus, the distinction between author and public is about to lose its basic character. The difference becomes merely functional; it may vary from case to case. At any moment the reader is ready to turn into a writer.*

Well, notwithstanding the fact that this passage seems prescient regarding our own time's burgeoning blogosphere, who doesn't find the "about to" in the sentence, "Thus, the distinction between author and public is about to lose its basic character," just a little grotesquely charming, emanating as it does from the year 1936 and from Central Europe. We have all viewed the film clips from Nazi Germany of gargantuan piles of books ablaze against a night sky, and Nazi citizens feeding those flames in a bacchanalian frenzy.

The "aura" of all books is a reflection of those flames, and has everything to do with a history in which people have given their lives to the meticulous copying, husbanding, and preservation of secret and forbidden texts, and of texts that were the very touchstones of ethnic and cultural identity. "The People of the Book" survived thousands of years of persecution and diaspora in no small part because of their reliance on and faith in the written word, and their faith in the books, sacred and profane, upon which they have built their fundamentally alienated yet indestructible identity. The book as an object to preserve, to keep, to cherish, even, goes to the heart of civilized life in a way that its disembodied information preserved and disseminated electronically never will. The soul/body dichotomy comes to mind. The book is the word made tangible, made flesh, if you will. Who touches a book, indeed, touches a human body. When I held my first little book, I held the body of my dead mother. I held the body of a child I would not come to know for eight years. I held the body of a woman I would love in twenty-five. I held the body of tragedy, and the body of comedy. I held nothing less than my own corporeal humanity.

Or so I felt for those first blissful, self-loving moments as I pulled my leg through the window and set both feet squarely upon the floor. As I stood there, in the House of Art, my little book was every book and I was every reader and every writer. My narcissism shaded to a profound humility, and I was happy.

Glenn Beck Is Not My Brother

"Intellectual activity is a danger to the building of character."
—Joseph Goebbels

How DO MOST OF US FIND ourselves on one side of the American culture war or the other? Some of us are born into such a powerful ideological current that we cannot help but be caught up and swept away, but often it's a matter of getting tugged down, from adolescence, by a subtle maelstrom of influences. How many of us have siblings or other family members who hold passionately to positions on the day's defining issues that are diametrically opposite our own? In most cases, we can point to this or that turn, one or another powerful influence, an individual or circumstance, as that which delivered a loved one up to the opposition. Yet, though we like to think that the arguments we marshal in the culture war are rational, the side of the conflict we muster on is rarely determined by reason, especially given that most of us stake out positions well before we've developed the intellectual apparatus necessary for mature, rational discourse. If I'd been "pro-life" as a kid, I might have been a father, twice, before my twentieth birthday. If I'd not been anti-war, I might have enlisted and died in Vietnam. If I'd been anti-drug, well, today I'd be the proud owner of many billions more sparking brain cells. I cannot imagine the circumstances of my present life if I'd been a staunch supporter of the Second

Amendment. We assume our values from others and from concrete circumstances, and only later learn to articulate and rationalize them, make them our own. The problem is that too few citizens accept it as a civic duty to analyze and articulate their core values post adolescence, I mean to reexamine their values on their own terms. There are various surrogate media voices for such folks these days.

Glenn Beck was a neo-Nazi ideologue who, while on the air at Fox News, dragged the untutored souls of the American Right into blind and savage rebellion against the forces of Progress and Sanity, and of course this characterization is quintessentially Beckian. Glenn Beck is not a neo-Nazi (strictly speaking), those who celebrate him are not (all) untutored, and they will not (likely) rise up in armed rebellion against the government, which is hardly a bastion of much that is good, anyway. The irrational posing as the rational is as old as political discourse. To Glenn Beck's credit, he makes the most outlandish subterfuge entertaining even or especially to those most offended by his antics. Being offended by Glenn Beck is simply taking one of the more juiced-up rides at the carnival of contemporary political commentary. Opinion as commodity is nothing new, but never has it come in so many delicious flavors.

What gives pause, though, is how similar to Joseph Goebbels's communication techniques are Beck's, which is to say the Far Right's. Goebbels, we may recall, took pride in having perfected what he himself dubbed the "Big Lie" style of propaganda, which is grounded in the assumption that a lie, if audacious enough and repeated frequently, will be believed by most folks. For Goebbels, simply to call someone "Jew" or "communist" was to demonize; likewise, Beck and his ilk call liberals/progressives, even moderates, "communists" or "Nazis" and they—liberals, et al.—must then march those epithets through the raging regard of Beck's constituency, few of whom understand even the ideological, much less the historical, differences between a communist and a Nazi. That most non-Jewish Germans of Goebbels's day knew virtually nothing about their Jewish neighbors' Jewishness goes without saying. Beck outrageously misnames; Goebbels negatively transformed and conflated the names of ethnic groups and political opposition.

Goebbels achieved his PhD in some form of literary studies in his mid-twenties; he wrote poetry and plays and such; he was an educated fellow whom some historians believe was not so much a True Believer as a cynical opportunist regarding Nazism. Beck wept publicly recounting how he'd been too poor to attend college, but assumed a professorial posture before a chalkboard that he covered with semi-literate absurdities. He is not nearly as bright as Goebbels was, though I have to believe that he is similarly cynical. Only cynicism accounts for what gushed from his talking head.

I've studied Glenn Beck on only a few painful occasions. I usually listened to other cable news/opinion shows (as I pecked at my laptop or read), all left leaning, which commented upon Beck, airing frequent clips of his chalkboard antics. He was an easy target for his critics; indeed, he was the St. Sebastian of talk media, but his ratings beat everyone else's. He made (I suppose that one may speak of him now, in pre-election 2012, in the past tense) a ton of money telling befuddled white people what they think they want to hear.

I, of course, indulge in a wicked apples/oranges comparison likening Glenn Beck to Joseph Goebbels; propaganda issuing directly from a state is of an entirely different nature from propaganda as commodity, though it's interesting to note that the culture war has its own military-industrial complex, which is the cozy relationship between the protean political establishment and the media. Across the ideological spectrum, political discourse gets, by turns, roiled and filtered and finally rendered, in the culinary as well as the usual sense. All information regarding power, which is all information not rooted in scientific fact, but that, too, in some contexts (the climate-change "debate," for example), becomes propaganda in the endless, ginned-up conflict between the Right and Left. One might wish a pox on both their houses, except that everyone's lives are literally at stake.

I suppose that to understand Glenn Beck's, the far right's, agenda is to understand the hearts and minds of a fair chunk of the American population, and such understanding is of no small value. When I assert that I am American, as one does for practical reasons, say, traveling abroad, I am announcing civic kinship with Glenn Beck and all who affirm him, whether I wish to or not, and, so, seeking better understanding of the Beckian mindset is in the interest of self-knowledge in the broadest sense. To feel the contours of the Beckian worldview is to understand more deeply my own identity as an American.

In transit, usually in airports and airport bars, I have had spirited, collegial conversations with men and women, fellow travelers in the literal sense, who proceed from conservative ideology. I do not think "conservative" is a dirty word; in many ways conservatism is a necessary counterweight to that which historically has grown government for the sake of growing it, and has stifled, at least impeded, positive entrepreneurial energy. That it is also tethered to a social agenda grounded in xenophobia and institutional racism, in the aggregate, unfortunately warps its corrective function. The traveling businessmen and business-women I have chatted with over cocktails, luggage at our feet, are usually sophisticated folks who may read Tom Clancy novels but are cultured in the way that Americans with degrees in Engineering, Business, or Computer Information Systems may be cultured: they are often astute students of popular culture who do not view it as something other and less than "culture." They leave academic highbrow stuff to its own devices, have attended one or two Broadway shows, watch TV discerningly, and understand business relations, business ethos, as the essence of human relations. They are fiscal conservatives, in league with, though at least slightly wary of, social conservatives, and loathe the IRS. They are pragmatic and believe in Progress. Some are religious, but quietly so.

I can drink and laugh and talk sports with those folks; they sniff my left-of-center worldview fairly quickly, and we silently agree to disagree as we chat each other up about Kobe Bryant, Floyd Mayweather, or Tiger Woods.

My guess is that my airport interlocutors watched Glenn Beck occasionally and found him amusing. He is their clown. He makes them shake their heads and laugh. I don't really know what they think about him because I've never brought him up in a conversa-tion, just as I've not brought up Rush Limbaugh, John Birch, or Elmer Fudd. But it is my guess that most international travelers, that is, folks who at least occasionally traverse the oceans out of fiscal necessity or otherwise, achieve a certain sophistication that dampens political passions, or at least mitigates chauvinism.

I have never understood how someone who hasn't traveled abroad can "love" her/his country. I understand and respect a warrior's love of country, but I don't understand the chauvinism of someone who has never been a soldier and has never lived, even for a few days, in another culture, unless such an individual feels country love for the humble sake of those who have sacrificed their lives, or, more to the historical point, were sacrificed.

My brother Chuck, a year and a half younger, was always much smaller than I, and quieter. I made friends; he was a loner. I played sports; he didn't. Eventually, I drank, smoked, and took drugs; he didn't. I was promiscuous; he was chaste. I got swept up in the anti-establishment, anti-war, anti-Nixon early seventies; he became a Sea Scout. I went to college on my own nickel; he joined the navy.

In more than thirty years, I've seen my brother on but two occasions. In the mid-eighties, he phoned and said that he'd be passing through New Orleans on his way to a navy school. I told him he could stay with me in my French Quarter apartment. I'd spoken with him perhaps two or three times since I'd moved out of our stepparents' house on my eighteenth birthday. He'd transitioned from the Sea Scouts to the navy within a couple years of my departure.

We'd slept in the same beds for years, later in the same rooms in separate beds. We'd sung in the dark before sleep, talked about everything. Through our teens, we'd argue politics in the dark before or after singing. By the time Watergate happened, we were already on our own, separated, so I could not throw Nixon in his face.

That first visit was a disaster. We argued passionately about the role of the military and Ronald Reagan's agenda. At some point, with no malice in his voice, only sad resignation, he called me a communist.

I was infuriated not because I thought that being a communist was on the order of being a pederast or a game show host, but because the moniker was simply inaccurate applied to me. I'd read a ton of Marx and Marxist commentaries; I'd read a ton of literary, social, and political theory. My politics shaded toward social democrat, but I did not buy the dictatorship of the proletariat or, generally, the notion of class warfare. We went to sleep angry; he left early. I did not see or speak to him again for more than twenty years.

In his early twenties, he married a woman a few years older than he and proceeded to sire five children. He received a good education in the navy, becoming an officer, retiring after thirty years as a lieutenant commander, just as our stepfather had. The last time I saw him he'd been retired from the navy for two or three years, and worked in the Pentagon. He'd just finished his Masters in some flavor of computer/systems analysis at the University of Maryland, where two of his children had recently graduated or were currently matriculating. After an awkward series of phone calls, it was decided that my two older daughters, Ema, then eighteen, and Annie, twelve, Krista, and I would visit his family for Thanksgiving, 2008.

He and I were careful to avoid any political discussions. I liked his family fine; his second daughter seemed a vivacious kid in her early twenties, recently graduated from college and working in a lab somewhere in DC, I think. Only his oldest daughter was absent; she'd joined the army, and she and her sol-dier husband had a new baby. Chuck's wife is from Mexico, and early on suffered our stepmother's/aunt's racist regard.

His family was coolly welcoming, the kids, all grown or nearly so, a little curious, but only a little. My girls were uncomfortable but polite.

I didn't like him and he didn't like me. We were tolerant of one another during a traditional Thanksgiving meal that my family later learned was atypical for Chuck's household; his wife, Theresa, usually cooked something authentically Mexican for Thanksgiving, and I, of course, would have loved such a meal.

I had discovered, much to my surprise and consternation, that my brother had not told his family the story of his childhood until very recently. He'd allowed them to believe that our uncle and aunt stepparents were his biological parents, that his cousins/siblings were his biological sisters and brother. The fact that his kids could so easily Google me and read my bio on my website, even order my memoirs from Amazon, persuaded him, he admitted, to come clean.

But it was clear he did not wish to reminisce. A couple of times I brought up this or that clouded recollection from our picaresque past, and he simply deflected it and changed the subject. I tried to get him to talk about his work at the Pentagon; he proffered a little information, obviously was proud of his work; I think he doubted the authenticity of my interest in any aspect of his life, much less his work, but my interest was genuine. I am not a communist. I have never advocated the violent overthrow of the American government. I was not judging him, or if I did it was without malice.

My brother is not Glenn Beck, and not just because he doesn't proselytize his far-right worldview for profit. He believes what he believes quietly and firmly. He is tolerant but sad that not everyone knows the truth he lives. My brother genuinely fears the destruction not only of America but also of western civilization. My brother detests Obama as president, but not because our president is of mixed race; he hates along ideological lines. My brother is

serious and thoughtful. His children and wife adore him, and he
has served his country with humble distinction. He doesn't laugh
much, but his kids, especially his spunky second daughter, make
him smile when they speak at the dinner table.

In my brother's office, obviously his sanctuary—it even
contains a little bed and TV—his navy stuff adorns his desk and
walls. I cannot recall the specific stuff that represents there his
thirty years of military service, except that I seem to recall his
service medals are mounted on a mahogany plaque on the wall
behind his desk, though this could be a false memory. The most
striking feature of his sanctuary is a large, framed photo of our
uncle/stepfather, Raymond, prominently hung high on the wall
beside a picture window. In the photo, Raymond wears his dress
uniform, his gold-braided hat, and stares stoically.

I'd seen that photograph; our aunt had kept it on her dresser in
their bedroom. In the late nineties I'd had a massive falling out
with our stepmother/aunt, so had not spoken to her in over a
decade. Because she ruled the man's home life, my not speaking
to her meant that I could not have contact with Raymond either.
When he died, Barbara instructed my first wife, with whom she
and I both maintained cordial relations, not to tell me that
Raymond had passed. When I discovered this, cordial relations
with my ex-wife ceased.

But Chuck maintained contact with our faux parents primarily
by telephone. That moment I saw Raymond's photo on Chuck's
wall I understood something about my brother I should have
known years earlier: his shame for our past crushed his heart; our
father crushed his heart. Raymond had never doted on him
though he had always been kind to both of us. A Kennedy
Democrat who became a staunch Republican, Raymond would sit

at the dinner table with us and talk for hours about politics, the deterioration of American culture, the American Dream. He and I would argue, always in civil tones, along ideological lines, and Chuck would remain quiet, for the most part, not because he wasn't articulate and opinionated, but because he delighted, for some reason, in Raymond's and my repartee. Raymond was incredibly, interminably long-winded, but Chuck and I would sit at the table with him after dinner and listen respectfully, basking in his regard.

He became Chuck's father as he could never be mine. Chuck assumed Raymond's worldview, his core values, his life. Chuck's childhood had been sorrow and chaos; he'd suffered, as I had not, I mean in his crushed heart. He was ashamed of our father, our mother, our lives on the road and in the projects. He was ashamed of being physically small, and suffered my largeness, my swagger, my lack of self-consciousness.

Chuck loved Raymond, needed him as a template for manhood. Chuck believes that invading Iraq was a good thing; if he'd lived, I'm sure that Raymond would think so, too. I believe, though can't be certain, that Chuck would nuke Iran under the "right" circumstances, and I remember Raymond in the early seventies opining fondly about tactical nuclear weapons. I'm not certain what Chuck's position on illegal immigration is, though given his familial ties to Mexico I am indeed curious. Whatever his position on that issue, he is definitely a law-and-order kind of guy. Does he support healthcare reform? It would not be fair to speculate as to what he may believe, given that I've never discussed the issue with him, though I should note I've always marveled at military "Lifers," enlisted men and women as well as officers, spewing libertarian views yet living (when they are not engaged in actual combat) within the coziest, most assuredly socialist structure on the planet. Socialized medicine is a given; subsidized food and sundry products are provided at the PX; subsidized housing is available to most; even fun is subsidized in the form of Enlisted and Officers' Clubs where alcohol is cheap and the music fine. It is a full-employment environment in which retirement is guaranteed, absolutely, for those who become Lifers. A paradox of the American military is that, combat notwithstanding, it's the safest life available in America, especially if one chooses it as a career, and I do not mean to make light of the thousands who have died or been egregiously injured in recent adventures abroad. I simply wish to point out the irony of career military personnel espousing classic Libertarian ideology or small-government low-tax corporate-friendly Republicanism, as so many do. By "safe" I mean, primarily, that companies go bankrupt, corporations crash, even universities fail as fiscal entities, but the US military will always exist.

It is also one of the great meritocracies, though many military folks will argue that when it fails it does so on this point; however, few would argue that race and ethnicity are not often a factor in the advancement of an individual's military career. Hot button issues notwithstanding, it certainly gave my brother structure and goals; it allowed him to earn self-esteem with which to repair his crushed heart. It allowed him to raise a family and see the world. It gave him a framework by which he could become a good man, like his father Raymond, by any fair standard of judgment.

My brother and people like him deserve more thoughtful media representation than Glenn Beck's. At this moment in history they deserve better than Fox News. They certainly deserve better than the plethora of hate-drenched blogs on the Internet. They deserve not to be painted with the same brush as Southern and small-town white people still smarting from the Civil Rights Act of 1964, some of whom are not even aware of something called the Civil Rights Act of 1964, but certain all the same that things were better a few decades ago, people who carry placards to rallies portraying a black president with a Hitler moustache, and decrying healthcare reform that is so obviously in their long-term interest.

In most discourses we preach primarily to the choir, and Glenn Beck is no exception (despite his ouster from Fox, he remains mighty on radio). Just as Beck knows his choir, his constituency, so Joe Goebbels knew his; the Big Lie only works when people want to believe it. Daniel Jonah Goldhagen argues in his mid-nineties groundbreaking, and wildly controversial, *Hitler's Willing Executioners* that German consciousness, all the way back to medieval times, fomented an "eliminationist anti-Semitism." As much as many historians would like to draw a distinction between Nazism and the German people, that distinction is tenuous at best, or, by Goldhagen's reckoning, nonexistent.

Glenn Beck reflects the cultural and political sentiments of ordinary Americans who possess passionate hearts tempered by a very American, and in some ways quite healthy, mistrust of Big Stuff: Big Government, Big Corporations (which they often inexplicably mix up with Big Government), Big Banks, Big (complicated, nuanced) Ideas. They mistrust authority that is not an Ultimate Authority. Their spirit is that which moved west in covered wagons, forming tiny isolated communities from the Alleghenies to the Pacific. So many white people in the South, the Midwest, and out West, with the weak exception of those living in or near university towns, exist in a state of self-conscious isolation. Electronic media don't mediate this isolation, or they mediate it in a problematic way.

I'm certain that my brother Chuck does not feel excluded from the sources of cosmopolitan vitality. When he entered the navy, the military was still hung over from Vietnam. All of his shipmates only a few years older than he had been defeated, and the diffuse remnants of the counterculture, to his mind the fifth column of that which had defeated his older colleagues, still roundly vilified the military. Over the course of his career, which included many foreign deployments and innumerable ports of call, he could not help but note the bitter irony of his working to protect those very individuals who, to his mind, hated him and everything he valued. He, of course, celebrated not the fall, but the defeat of communism. And there is not one scintilla of doubt in his heart that the "War on Terror" is of even greater import than the Cold War. Both the Right and the Left have fault lines along isolationist and internationalist tendencies. My brother is an internationalist, that is, a neoconservative. Though Beck's legions celebrate neocon initiatives, they do so against the grain of their essential native-ism. My brother and I have in common internationalist perspectives from opposing ideological value systems. I am no doubt more vacillating in my perspective than he is in his. Especially given my familial connection to the Czech Republic, I sometimes think of Neville Chamberlain and waver.

I also know what it's like to fall through an ideological looking glass. An adherent of some form of "socialism with a human face," as poor Dubček dubbed the soul of the Prague Spring, in the weeks preceding the Velvet Revolution I tasted one-party totalitarianism and witnessed a people's rise out of it. I stood at a window once in the late nineties chatting with the great Czech writer and Holocaust survivor Arnošt Lustig. After a long sigh he said, apropos of nothing in our light conversation as we awaited the rest of our dinner party, "They fucked up a beautiful idea for a hundred years." Lustig left the Party over Israel, to which he emigrated before settling in the States, then returning to Prague after 1989. To hear him argue, in the splendid documentary *The Fighter*, with a contemporary Czech Jew, Jan Weiner, about Lustig's decision to join the Communist Party at a time, after the war, when it was torturing and killing the same Czech Jews who had escaped to England to fight the Nazis in the Royal Air Force, is transformative. After spending his teen years in death camps, he found the promise of Communism was indeed beautiful, and he simply did not know that Jews like Weiner were being persecuted out of an outrageous paranoia that they were English spies. Weiner and Lustig, who both died only lately, were brothers who could never see eye to eye, but their conflict had as context suffering that is beyond the pale of comprehension. Their conflict, beyond bitterness, beyond ego, was heroic and humane.

Those three years we lived in the projects, 1963 to 1966, I was never home in the summer months except to sleep. I ranged over the sprawling projects, had many friends and therefore many adventures. When I wasn't playing baseball or working in the yards of African-American homeowners to make money, I sat in a field and read books and comics. From what I earned working in yards, I could buy stuff to eat as well as new comics. I saw my brother very little. The only socializing he ever did was as a Boy Scout. We joined at the same time; I made Tenderfoot, but was soon kicked out for fighting. Chuck climbed as high as Star Scout, just before Life Scout, which is just before Eagle, and was indeed the star of the cookie-selling drive his scout leader, a chief petty officer, deftly organized. That one social outlet was ripped from him, however, when his scout leader ran off with the thousand-plus dollars Chuck and the other boys had hustled door to door in their ratty, second-hand uniforms.

I have no memories of early childhood that do not include him. When I was three and he one and a half, instead of napping we climbed out a window of an apartment the family would remain in for no more than a few weeks, because we never stayed anywhere for longer than a few weeks, usually no more than a few days. It was a hot day, so our mother had put us down naked. We sat in red dirt—we must have been somewhere in Georgia—bare-assed, in the cool shadow of the building, and stared into a stand of trees in the distance. I remember, I swear, that we spoke. I remember chattering, as babies will, with my bubu, as I called him. We sat naked in red dirt and stared into trees and tried to communicate.

About the Author

Born November 4, 1953, in Norfolk, Virginia, Richard Katrovas, the oldest of five children, spent his early years in cars and motels living on the highways of America while his father, a petty thief and conman, eluded state and federal authorities. His father was eventually caught, but upon being released from federal prison reverted to his criminal ways, and was caught and incarcerated again. During his father's prison terms, Katrovas and his mother and siblings lived on welfare in public housing projects.

Katrovas was adopted by relatives in his early teens, and lived with them for three years in Sasebo, Japan, where he earned a second-degree black belt in Shobukan Okinawa-te Karate. He graduated from high school in Coronado, California, and attended San Diego State University (BA, English, 1977). He was then a Hoyns Fellow at the University of Virginia, attended the MFA program at the University of Arkansas, and finished his graduate work in the Iowa Writers' Workshop (MFA, 1983). Between 1970 and 1983, Katrovas taught karate and worked in numerous restaurants in San Diego, then New Orleans.

On a Fulbright fellowship, Katrovas was in Prague, Czechoslovakia in the months preceding the Velvet Revolution, and subsequently witnessed that event. The recipient of numerous grants and awards, Katrovas is the founding director of the Prague Summer Program, and is the author of seven books of poetry, including *Green Dragons* (winner of the Wesleyan University Press New Poets Series), *Snug Harbor* (Wesleyan), *The Public Mirror* (Wesleyan), *The Book of Complaints* (Carnegie Mellon University Press), *Dithyrambs* (Carnegie Mellon), and *Scorpio Rising: Selected Poems.* Other books include the short story collection *Prague USA* (Portals Press) and two memoirs *The Years of Smashing Brick* (Carnegie Mellon University Press) and *The Republic of Burma Shave* (Carnegie Mellon University Press). His novels include *The Mystic Pig* (Smallmouth Press); and *Prague Winter.* As guest editor of a special double issue of *The New Orleans Review*, Katrovas edited, and participated in much of the translation of, the first representative anthology of contemporary Czech poetry, *Ten Years After the Velvet Revolution.* His poems, stories, reviews, and essays have appeared widely in magazines and anthologies.

Katrovas is married to the yogini Krista Katrovas and has three daughters, Ema, Annie, and Ellie. He and his family live in Kalamazoo, Michigan, New Orleans, and Prague. Katrovas taught for twenty years at the University of New Orleans and is now a professor of English at Western Michigan University.

Recent and Forthcoming Books from Three Rooms Press

PHOTOGRAPHY-MEMOIR

Mike Watt
On & Off Bass

FICTION

Ron Dakron
Hello Devilfish!

Michael T. Fournier
Hidden Wheel
Swing State

Janet Hamill
Tales from the Eternal Café
(Introduction by Patti Smith)

Eamon Loingsigh
Light of the Diddicoy

Richard Vetere
The Writers Afterlife

DADA

Maintenant:
Journal of Contemporary
Dada Art & Literature
(Annual poetry/art journal,
since 2008)

MEMOIR & BIOGRAPHY

Nassrine Azimi and
Michel Wasserman
Last Boat to Yokohama:
The Life and Legacy of
Beate Sirota Gordon

Richard Katrovas
Raising Girls in Bohemia:
Meditations of an American
Father; A Memoir in Essays

Stephen Spotte
My Watery Self:
An Aquatic Memoir

SHORT STORY ANTHOLOGY

Have a NYC:
New York Short Stories
Annual Short Fiction Anthology

PLAYS

Madeline Artenberg &
Karen Hildebrand
The Old In-and-Out

Peter Carlaftes
Triumph For Rent (3 Plays)
Teatrophy (3 More Plays)

MIXED MEDIA

John S. Paul
Sign Language:
A Painters Notebook

TRANSLATIONS

Thomas Bernhard
On Earth and in Hell
(poems by the author
in German with English
translations by Peter Waugh)

Patrizia Gattaceca
Isula d'Anima / Soul Island
(poems by the author
in Corsican with English
translations)

César Vallejo | Gerard Malanga
Malanga Chasing Vallejo
(selected poems of César Vallejo
with English translations and additional notes by Gerard Malanga)

George Wallace
EOS: Abductor of Men
(poems by the author in English
with Greek translations)

HUMOR

Peter Carlaftes
A Year on Facebook

POETRY COLLECTIONS

Hala Alyan
Atrium

Peter Carlaftes
DrunkYard Dog
I Fold with the Hand I Was Dealt

Thomas Fucaloro
It Starts from the Belly and Blooms
Inheriting Craziness is Like
a Soft Halo of Light

Kat Georges
Our Lady of the Hunger

Robert Gibbons
Close to the Tree

Israel Horovitz
Heaven and Other Poems

David Lawton
Sharp Blue Stream

Jane LeCroy
Signature Play

Philip Meersman
This is Belgian Chocolate

Jane Ormerod
Recreational Vehicles on Fire
Welcome to the Museum of Cattle

Lisa Panepinto
On This Borrowed Bike

George Wallace
Poppin' Johnny

Three Rooms Press | New York, NY | Current Catalog: www.threeroomspress.com
Three Rooms Press books are distributed by PGW/Perseus: www.pgw.com